FROM THE
FACTORY
FLOOR

ISBN: 9798741424513
Independently published

Copyright tsf.tech Limited 2021.
hello@thestartupfactory.tech

This book was produced in collaboration with Write Business Results
Limited. For more information on their business book, blog and podcast
services, please visit www.writebusinessresults.com or contact the team via
info@writebusinessresults.com.

 WRITE BUSINESS RESULTS

FROM THE FACTORY FLOOR

WE BUILD TECH COMPANIES

BY THE TSF.TECH TEAM AND ASSOCIATES

the
startup
factory

CONTENTS

Dedication   7

Foreword   9

PART 1: GETTING OFF THE GROUND

1. Ideation, Prototyping and Testing   13
   Ian Brookes

2. Minimum Viable Product   23
   Eric Carter

3. Tech Vision and Product Roadmapping   33
   Aleksa Vukotic

4. Startup Sprint   47
   Ian Brookes

5. Software Architecture   59
   Aleksa Vukotic

6. Cloud Tech 101   75
   Aleksa Vukotic

PART 2: DELIVERING ON THE PROMISE

7. Tech Choices   93
   Eric Carter

8. Engineering Process   105
   Eric Carter

9. Building the Tech Team   117
   Aleksa Vukotic

10. Agile Project Management   127
    James Brookes

11. The Importance of Culture   139
    Guy Remond

PART 3: IN IT FOR THE LONG HAUL

12. Marketing on a Shoestring   151
    Guy Remond

13. Not Just an Accountant   157
    Elliot Smith

14. Financial Advice   169
    Simon Booth

15. Legal Building Blocks   181
    Jonathan Davage

16. The Value of a Non-Exec Director   195
    Ian Brookes

17. Entrepreneurial War Stories: Badges and Scars   205
    Guy Remond

18. Closing Thoughts   213

    About the Authors   221
    Appendix   225

DEDICATION

It was in 1978 that Tony Wilson, Rob Gretton and Alan Eramus founded Factory Records in Manchester, quickly joined by Martin Hannett and Peter Saville. Wilson started the company with the inheritance of £12,000 from his mum. He based it in the Russell Club in Moss Side, and released their first EP, *A Factory Sampler*, featuring acts that played at the club, in 1979.

Factory Records was an entrepreneurial tour de force as a collection of ideas, just as Manchester had emerged originally in the 19th century. The 20th-century version was invented by a rousing collective of dreamers, schemers, writers and musicians. It gave amplification to a sense of an audacious soundtrack of innovation and disruption that has always been the hallmark of Manchester.

Talking Heads' guitarist, Tina Weymouth, once remarked of Factory: *'I grew up in New York in the Seventies, and I've seen a lot of people who live life on the edge, but I've never before seen a group of people who had no idea where the edge is.'*

With that 'Do-It-Yourself' mindset, they made it up as they went along. Like a startup, they had to find their market, experiment, work out where their audience was. The founders never rested on their laurels, they retained their spirit, drive and passion. And that's what every entrepreneur does too.

Of the founders, Wilson, Gretton and Hannett are no longer with us, having all died young, but the legacy of Factory remains. *'Mutability is the epitaph of worlds, change alone is changeless. People drop out of the history of a life as of a land, though their work or their influence remains'* – the words on Wilson's tombstone in Southern Cemetery. That's a great epitaph to inspire the ongoing spirit of entrepreneurship in Manchester.

And that's our starting point. Hewn with the same Mancunian ambition, our company name, logo and spirit are inspired by the entrepreneurial endeavour of Factory Records. Despite many uncommercial decisions and the ultimate failure, Factory remains a moment of time in music and Manchester's history of innovative startup ventures. We dedicate this book to their thirst for innovation and making it happen. In Manchester.

Ian Brookes
tsf.tech
May 2021

FOREWORD

We were once an economy of factories. Now we're an economy of ideas. The factory was a place of innovation. It converted cotton to cloth, grain to flour, ore to steel. The factory changed the landscape of our economy once. It started in Manchester. Now we're doing it again. In tech. In Manchester.

thestartupfactory.tech helps innovators and early-stage startups to get off the ground. In our team of experienced entrepreneurs and tech mavens, we've crafted a passion-driven, collaborative approach and philosophy to nurturing business creation, partnering with founders for their tech startup journey. Our goal is to build tech startup products and help founders execute their business strategy in an agile, fast and focused way. It is our contribution to creating a flourishing startup ecosystem. In Manchester.

During the past decades, Manchester has spawned hundreds of tech startups. Our ability to innovate, build iconic companies, create new jobs and inspire the world – as Manchester has always done – is down to the spirit and endeavour of entrepreneurs taking chances on a dream to start a business. After all, the story of Manchester has always been the story of people going against the grain to imagine a better tomorrow.

If you have a good idea and are willing to work hard and see it through, you can succeed. But along the way, you need some help, and it's exactly because of that desire to provide this help that we wanted to write this book. It's a narrative, providing insight on the how, what and why to focus, prioritise, manage and do stuff for startup ventures.

Don't sit back waiting for a big plan to be done: get going, start planning, start thinking, and do whatever part that is going to help you run your business better. In this book, we share our experience and insight, and we explain how to start and build a startup around a core framework of essentials. And that's why you should read this book.

Our book aims to capture the *entrepreneur's essentials*, helping entrepreneurs launch and build better and more successful tech startups. It is impossible (and quite inappropriate) to try to tell the entire startup roadmap to success in a single book on entrepreneurship. What we've tried to do is capture all the 'must haves' and invite you to dig in and digest.

As President Harry Truman said, *'Not all readers are leaders, but all leaders are readers'*, so be both. One of the things I learned in my career was that whenever I got stuck, the company would also get stuck. Whenever I broke out of any dysfunctional patterns, then it freed the company to do the same. So, I constantly read a lot to learn from others.

We hope this book is a catalyst for fellow entrepreneurs as we share the learnings we have gleaned over the years. I believe you will find great value in this book and I hope you really enjoy it. In Manchester, obviously.

Ian Brookes
tsf.tech
May 2021

PART I

GETTING
OFF
THE
GROUND

I

IDEATION, PROTOTYPING AND TESTING

IAN BROOKES

INTRODUCTION

Initial startup strategy is all about making bets, experimentation and the problem you're seeking to solve. It's about ideation, build-measure-learn, and creating an idea-prototype-data feedback loop — a game of strategy and tactics, like a game of poker or chess.

You can't craft a strategy without testing your hypothesis for problem-solution fit with potential customers first, and then taking this validated learning into a pivot for product-market fit. From this, a go-to-market strategy and business model can be roadmapped.

So, looking to the horizon for your startup, what's your strategic approach? Among all of the analogies I've heard, one word has always jumped out at me: 'bet'. I've heard people use the words 'bootstrap', 'initiatives', and 'OKRs', but 'bet' captures it best, the interplay between experiments, unknowns, risks and outcomes.

The reality is, a startup has more in common with poker than you may think. There's a random nature to success — only 20% of startups get to a five-year anniversary — and learning how to bet and make your moves is vital when it comes to your venture, as there are things you can do to improve your odds. To quote Nassim Taleb in *The Black Swan*[1]: 'The strategy for discoverers and

---

1   Taleb Nassim, 11 May 2010, *The Black Swan: The Impact Of The Highly Improbable*, Penguin

entrepreneurs is to rely less on top-down planning and to focus on maximum tinkering and recognising opportunities when they present themselves.'

When launching your startup, the decisions you make will involve some luck and the occasional bluff, both important elements in poker. And in both startups and poker, you might not control the cards, but you can control how you play the game of chance. And how you play should be strategically and tactically, like in chess.

MAKING BETS

A bet can be tactical or strategic. Product decisions are bets. Sales negotiations are bets. Hiring is a bet. In these decisions, we're betting against all the alternative outcomes that we are not choosing. By calling it a bet, we are admitting that it may work out and it may not – losing is an option.

Time frames matter too: how long before we know if the bet has paid off? Placing small bets with a short time frame can give us information that can clarify the odds for larger bets, reducing risk.

You can make concurrent bets too, but making too many bets at once can be risky and divide your attention. Equally, you can't win much if you spend all your time at the penny slots; at some point you have to pull up a chair at the high stakes table. Each time you release an update to your product you're playing a hand of poker. The combination of funding and your burn rate determines the number of hands you get to play.

The way to maximise your odds is to pay close attention to all the responses to all of your moves. Everything is a test. Every bit of feedback is a signal. You need to look at what's working and discard what isn't. When we work backwards from results to figure out why something happened, we need to avoid cognitive bias traps, cherry-picking data to confirm the narrative we want to be true. We all at times push square pegs into round holes in order to convince ourselves that we're right.

IMAGINE YOUR STARTUP AS A GAME OF POKER

So, imagine your startup as a game of poker. During a game, you make decisions quickly without knowing all of the facts: you don't know the other players' cards, you don't know which cards are going to be turned over next, and you don't know how the other players at the table will bet or play. Decisions need to be made on every hand in quick succession.

With a poker player's hat on, we should adopt the betting mindset to determine which scenarios would likely play out in our game of startups. Generally, in every poker hand, thinking about what other players have and what their move could likely be determines what you will bet and how you will react. Can you do the same for your startup strategy?

Great poker players are thinking about not only what their opponents' next move will be, but the next four hands after that too. It makes a lot of sense to start looking at your startup decisions and the potential outcomes of those decisions in the same way. Of course, you end up with competing voices in your head, each saying how they would play it; the true information remains hidden but, as James Clerk Maxwell, the great physicist said, 'Thoroughly conscious ignorance is the prelude to every real advance.'

What good poker players and great entrepreneurs have in common is their comfort with uncertainty and unpredictable circumstances. They understand that they can never know exactly how something will turn out. They embrace that uncertainty and, instead of trying to be sure, they try to figure out how unsure they are, making their best guess based on the likelihood that different outcomes will occur.

Takeaway: The future does not exist. It's only a range of possibilities. Every decision commits you to some course of action that, by definition, eliminates the alternatives. Not placing a bet on something is, in itself, a bet.

HOW TO MAKE YOUR STARTUP BETS

Let's adopt the poker player's mindset, how should we make startup bets?

ACKNOWLEDGE UNCERTAINTY

Making better decisions starts with understanding that uncertainty can work a lot of mischief. We are generally discouraged from saying *'I don't know'* or *'I'm not sure';* we regard those expressions as vague, unhelpful and even evasive. But getting comfortable with *I'm not sure* is a vital step to better decision-making.

I'm not sure is simply a more accurate representation of reality. When we accept that we can't be sure, we are less likely to fall into the trap of black-and-white thinking. We move away from holding just two opposing and discrete boxes that decisions can be put in – right or wrong – and can calibrate among the shades of grey.

OPEN YOUR MIND TO ALL POSSIBLE OPTIONS

The startup world is a pretty random place. If we don't change our mindset, we're going to have to deal with being wrong a lot. We become so focused on the immediate situation that we overlook the range of possibilities. This can lead to us making rash decisions or missing opportunities because we don't recognise when they come along.

There is always a context beyond what we initially thought, with more possibilities than we envisioned. With a broader mindset we can counter the discomfort of uncertainty with greater optimism. Rather than focusing on digging yourself out of a range of worst-case scenarios, recognise that there are positive possibilities too.

THINK IN TERMS OF PROBABILITIES, NOT BINARY OUTCOMES

Human nature means we often spiral into imagining extreme outcomes. But the poker player thinks in probabilities. Thinking in binary terms creates anxiety, not options. But when instead we consider the full range of possible outcomes and assign probabilities to them, we see things differently. This reminds me of French philosopher Michel de Montaigne's wry observation: 'My life has been full of terrible misfortunes, most of which never happened.'

THROW THE THINKING FORWARD

Suzy Welch[2] developed a popular tool known as '10–10–10' that has the effect of bringing the future into our in-the-moment decision-making. Her 10–10–10 process starts with a question: 'What are the consequences of each of my options in 10 days? In 10 weeks? In 10 months?' Proceeding this way reduces the weight we give to emotions in the moment and brings more rationality to the decision-making process, considering all the outcomes carefully.

LUCK PLAYS A PART, LIKE IT OR NOT

No one has done more thinking regarding the impact of luck on making decisions than Michael Mauboussin. He states that 'it is rea-

---

2 Welch Suzy, 1 April 2009, *10-10-10: 10 Minutes, 10 Months, 10 Years: A Life Transforming Idea*, Scribner

sonable to expect that a different outcome could have occurred'. Mauboussin points out, 'There's a quick and easy way to test whether an activity involves skill: ask whether you can lose on purpose. In games of skill, it's clear that you can lose intentionally, but when playing roulette or the lottery you can't lose on purpose[3].'

> *Takeaway: As the poker player knows, some things are unknown or unknowable. The influence of luck and all the hidden information makes things more difficult. Hope is not a strategy, but a strategy gives you hope, so make your startup strategy a series of bets, and know when to play and when to withdraw.*

NOW, LET'S PLAY STARTUP CHESS

So far so good. You've got your startup strategy thinking into shape around making bets. We need to keep a forward-looking mindset. We'll have hunches, insights and hopefully some foresight, but we also need to have some discipline and structure in our thinking and approach too.

Garry Kasparov, grandmaster and former World Chess Champion, shared how he combined disruptive and disciplined approaches to bring him success in chess in his book *How Life Imitates Chess*. It's a must-read for chess players and entrepreneurs alike.

Kasparov highlights the importance of combining long-term strategy and short-term tactics, and how important learning and decision-making are at any stage of the game. Adopting this mindset, we need to think ahead in business, truly thinking through our options and the consequences – that's not calculating, it's common sense.

---

3 Mauboussin Michael, 6 November 2012, The Success Equation: Untangling Skill and Luck in Business, Sports, and Investing, Harvard Business Review Press

Kasparov illustrates that the subtle and intricate potential moves that lie within the 64 squares of a chessboard are totally applicable to business, and how the game can help you step back and evaluate yourself in order to identify your strengths and weaknesses, and thus better your game.

Chess is really about psychology and intuition because the mathematics get complex very quickly. For me, the main takeaway of chess to startups is the ability to execute strategy, which can be exploited through practice and repetition.

MAKE YOUR MOVE

So what are the entrepreneurial learnings we can take from Kasparov's thinking to complement our poker-playing, bet-making swagger, and ensure we balance experimentation with execution? Hope is not a strategy. Chess is eminently and emphatically a philosopher's game: it will balance the risk-taking appetite you've developed from the poker player's style, so let's translate Kasparov's chess strategies into clear startup strategic thinking.

THE FIRST PHASE IN A CHESS GAME: THE OPENING

The purpose of the opening isn't just to get through it; it's to set the stage for the type of middle game you want. The openings are the only phase in which there is the possibility of unique application, you can find something that no one else has found. Be first and be brave is the lesson for startups.

THE SECOND PHASE: THE MIDDLE GAME

What sort of middle game is our opening going to lead to? Is it one we are prepared for? We must also play the middle game with an eye on the endgame. After a bad opening, there is still hope for the middle game. After a bad middle game, there may still be hope for the endgame. But once you are in the endgame, the moment of truth has arrived. In a startup, it's important to have a strategy, tactics and a game plan.

THE BEST NEXT MOVE

The best next move on the board might be so obvious that it's not necessary to spend time working out the details, especially if time is of the essence. However, often when we assume something is obvious and react hastily, we are being complacent and may be making a mistake. So, what is your best next move, and the best move after that?

Chess is a struggle against the error. Generally we should break routine by doing more analysis, not less. There are moments when your instincts tell you that there is something lurking below the surface, so take a moment to figure out what's really going on.

THE FUTURE IS A RESULT OF THE DECISIONS YOU MAKE IN THE PRESENT

'Tactics' means knowing what to do when there is something to do; 'strategy' means knowing what to do when there is nothing to do. A chess grandmaster makes the best moves based on what they want the board to look like in 20 moves' time.

This doesn't require the calculation of countless 20-move variations, but an evaluation of where their fortunes lie in the position and established objectives. They work out the step-by-step moves to accomplish those aims. You should adopt this approach for your startup. Have a vision of success, clarity and focus in your strategy.

INTUITION AND ANALYSIS

Half the variations that are calculated in a chess game turn out to be completely superfluous. Unfortunately, no one knows in advance which half. Even the most honed intuition can't entirely do without analysis. Intuition is where it all comes together – our experience, knowledge and judgement – but it doesn't matter how far ahead you can see if you're not sure what you're looking at. So combine the two: no matter how much practice you have and how much you trust your gut instincts, analysis is essential.

ATTACK

An attack doesn't have to be all-or-nothing or lightning quick. Sustained pressure can be very effective, and mounting a slow, long-term attack can lead to a win in the long run. Going on the front-foot requires perfect timing as well as nerve. The window of opportunity is often very small, as with most dynamic situations, so balance opportunity with rationality – that combination of freedom and discipline in your game plan.

STAY DISCIPLINED

This is good advice. With an established culture of discipline, you will be in a better position for any shock to the business. This means balancing your appetite for risk with a need to achieve some planned outcomes.

When people talk about entrepreneurship being tough, this is what they mean. It's a true rollercoaster ride. Chess is the struggle against the error, one bad move nullifies the previous 20 good ones; the blunders are all out on the board waiting to be made, it's how you navigate through them that makes the difference.

Chess is a mental game: less a game of chance, more a game of executing a plan. Poker by contrast is a game of chance: the possible outcomes are vast and you can't cover them all, there are too many unknowns. But both games require vision, tenacity, thoughtfulness and smart tactics, just like making a success of your startup.

TAKEAWAYS

- Startup strategy is a combination of disruptive and disciplined approaches – of poker and chess.

- The future doesn't exist yet; it's a range of possibilities. Every decision is a bet which commits us to some course of action that eliminates the alternatives. Not making a decision is itself placing a bet (usually a bad one).

- Hope is not a strategy, but a strategy gives you hope when faced with the unknown, so make your startup strategy a series of calculated bets, and know when to play and when to withdraw.

- Both chess and startups are about the ability and discipline to execute strategy well, which can be improved through practice and repetition.

2

MINIMUM VIABLE PRODUCT

ERIC CARTER

INTRODUCTION

I've done it. I've seen founders do it. And you will have done it. We have a great idea. Then we change it, grow it and extend it. Quite quickly our initial idea has grown into a huge, towering, powerful and magnificent beast.

Few established companies and no startups could build it all at once, the most obvious and immediate reason being a finite supply of resources: people, time and money. But there are other reasons not to dive straight into building your full vision as well, which we'll explore in this chapter. The minimum viable product, or MVP, is the realisation of this understanding: it is the feature set that is complete enough, and no more.

In this chapter, I'd like to share a few techniques, lessons and stories to help you wide-eyed, enthusiastic tech entrepreneurs to start your own journey to building a solid, valued and successful product.

Before we begin let me apologise. I will not be able to provide an off-the-shelf solution or lay out a fool-proof set of instructions to follow. There is no single MVP template for all startups and all projects. In fact, there isn't even a single answer for your one perfect idea. Every startup will have its own unique approach, requirements and priorities.

For example: a fintech platform must have certain security and audit features to gain regulatory compliance; a high-tech scientific lab system may need to expose all raw data but be less concerned about styling; a low-tech consumer service may need a slick, immersive user experience to stand out and compete in a busy market. At thestartupfactory.tech we are in the privileged position of having built MVPs with startups in many domains. We have built products that worked and products that have struggled to take off, and we have the benefit of experience and hindsight to share.

PRIORITISING

Founders usually have a realistic expectation that they need to prioritise, but often find it hard to let go of some parts of their ideal application. When something exists in your mind or in reality, it is easy to see what could be lost when you make a change, but it is hard to anticipate how people and the world will adapt and respond – this makes people quite conservative. It is far too easy to say, 'This is important, that is important, and that thing is really important; we need them all.'

For that reason, the first bit of concrete advice I will give to you is to not use MoSCoW ratings (Must have, Should have, Could have, Won't have) or numbered priorities such as, 'These are priority 1 and those are priority 2, etc.' Instead, put items into an ordered list forcing you to make a decision. Does this feature go above or below that feature? It is easier to compare concrete things directly, and there is less anxiety than when pushing something into a low-priority group, making the process quicker and more valuable.

Don't fret too much about the decision if it's not obvious: if two items are close enough to debate their relative ordering, then there will be very little difference in the outcomes of doing one before the other. You can also gloss over the lower-priority items: if something is not near the top of the list, chances are that by the time you get around to implementing it, your circumstances will have changed and you'll want to revise your list anyway.

To help with the process of scoping your MVP, think of it as prioritising rather than as descoping unimportant features: you are not necessarily saying that feature X is not valuable, but rather that feature Y is the key to unlocking feature X, and that feature X can be added soon afterwards.

THE IMPORTANCE OF MVP SCOPE

My wife and I have been looking for a new house. To be honest this is a slightly one-sided search as I'll be loath to leave my large garden and workshop. Nevertheless, we found a few nice-looking places on a popular website and used the estate agent's online viewing booking tool. A simple – arguably MVP – process. Select property, enter desired viewing date and time, and press submit.

We did this and a few minutes later we received an SMS message saying 'declined'. Oh, well let's try a different time slot, and whilst we're at it let's book a viewing on a different property. Again, some minutes later two more SMS messages arrive: 'Accepted', 'Declined'. The wife is now getting flustered, and rightly so, because we can't tell which viewing was accepted, and for the other house we don't know whether it's worth trying a different time on the same day, or whether the vendors are away for the week. Fortunately a little later in the day a backlog of emails arrived; the emails have more information, including the vendor's direct response stating their actual availability.

The problems we encountered with this booking system neatly demonstrate the consequences of not effectively considering your MVP scope. The estate agents prioritised having both SMS and email notifications over creating a considered and coherent user journey. Consequently, they created a platform with a bad user experience that has harmed their reputation and dissuaded us from using this agent to sell our property.

COMPLEXITY

Scoping an MVP is all about your diligence and strength of character. It's so easy to think, 'This is just a simple feature, let's add it in.' But complexity does not build linearly: it compounds, permutations upon permutations. The estate agent story is a warning of what can happen.

Imagine yourself sitting in on a meeting between the estate agent manager and the developer. The manager says, 'Clients are often out and about, I think we need to add SMS notifications in case they can't access their emails.' The developer quickly responds, 'Easy job, just hook this event into that API and jobs-a-good'un.' It sounds like a reasonable business case: it won't take long to add, the developer says it's straightforward. What is your take? Should they add it in?

I have certainly been persuaded in the past. But always remember that even the simplest things are always more complicated than they appear. The estate agent and the developer did not initially realise that they wouldn't be able to include the full email content in the small SMS size limit, or that one or the other would always be received first and acted on by the recipient.

They perhaps didn't think outside of the box: they planned the user workflow of buyer requests viewing, vendor accepts, buyer notified; but they didn't think through the possibility that the buyer might make multiple requests at once, and they built a service that confused the hell out of us.

MVP MISTAKES

Before entering into the startup industry, I worked in big corporate consulting on large projects for multinationals and governments. While much of this work environment was the antithesis of startup culture, the idea of MVP and of focusing your effort in the most intelligent way was equally important here too. And I have found that many of the mistakes large organisations make are the same as those made by startups.

While working for a major telco client, we had to integrate with their customer database using basic name and address details. The requirements were quite strict, specifying validation rules for first name, last name and postcode fields. We dutifully went about our work implementing the system against the requirements, and we created automated tests demonstrating the behaviour for valid and invalid cases. But when we came to the integration testing phase, things started to go awry.

The first issue was bad requirements. We all know what postcodes look like: they are well defined, there is a limited number of them, it should be pretty easy to validate something so structured. But it turns out that there are a few special postcodes that don't quite fit the normal pattern, and these were not covered by the requirements. The second issue was the data quality and a dose of unconscious bias. The test data we made up for first name and last name were things like Joe Bloggs, Bat Man, and Bart Simpson. We didn't think to include double-barrelled names or Asian or Middle Eastern names which often have a different order or structure (I have no idea how the artist formerly known as Prince used to fill in first/last name forms!).

The other main issue was the existing data. It turns out that if you get a million customers to fill in their first and last names you will get thousands of 'wrong' entries, things like: first name 'Mr', last name 'North Street' or 'as above', or simply transposing first and last names. Due to the validation violations for both postcode and name fields in the existing database, we had to remove or dial back almost all the validation specified in the requirements. In other words, the time spent writing the requirements, implementing the rules, creating the tests, debugging the issues and holding meetings, plus the indirect overheads of delays, were all a waste that added no value to the system.

We can identify a number of mistakes from this experience:

- **Mistake 1:** Because it was ultimately deemed acceptable to remove the validation, there was obviously no real need for such strict validation. The requirements were generated by over-engineering the solution. There is a very fine line between taking sensible precautions that enhance the robustness of a system and over-engineering. Individuals and teams over-engineer for a number of commercial and psychological reasons: the need to provide value, legal worries, job satisfaction or just doing extra bits that are fun. Being consciously aware of this and remembering to prioritise delivery should keep you on track.

- **Mistake 2:** The project included too much detail and refinement from the beginning, when the understanding of the user and system interactions was at its least developed.

- **Mistake 3:** The project took the assumptions made in the requirements and passed straight through into final development. There was no prototyping or testing activity to validate, disprove or refine the assumptions. In this case especially, it would have been reasonably quick to validate some of these assumptions with the existing data set.

- **Mistake 4:** The solution was overly complex. By separating the name into two fields when one would probably have been enough, we had doubled the work, introduced issues of cultural dissonance, and increased the scope for user error. Arguably for this project the name split was necessary due to the existing data set. But for your startup, do you really need first and last names? What are you actually using them for? Is another approach possible, such as adding instructions to clarify the desired format without shutting out diverse sectors of society by enforcing a certain pattern?

DON'T GO FOR TOO MUCH TOO SOON

Asking your users 'Would you like this feature?' will usually result in a 'Yes, please', but once you've built it, it may well turn out that it just sounded interesting and does not really fit into your users' day-to-day activities, so is hardly being used.

Just think about all the nested menus, settings and preferences in big software packages. How many additional customers does each one bring compared to the exponential increase in complexity, development, maintenance and documentation effort? Startups need to focus on the big wins that gain them a significant user base. Once you have established a core customer base, you can start looking at expanding the options and features to win over the customers who need a little something extra to come on board.

The modern scalable approach for this is to outsource it to the user community by publishing a plugin API or a REST or other web API. For many startups, taking this step too soon is risky because API-breaking changes can be common until the startup has matured and settled.

Recently thestartupfactory.tech engaged with one entrepreneur aiming to build a video streaming service. The founder had a grand plan and business model that relied on scale. They came armed with a prototype of how they imagined the system would work, including a novel UX approach to allow their users to glide swiftly over the oceans of content, landing gently on the island they needed.

There was nothing wrong with the idea, except that the timing was off. At launch they would not have oceans of content; they expected this to grow as they marketed and expanded the business side. If we built those features as requested, we would be spending valuable time on a complex system that would not be justified until the content puddle grows into a lake.

Worse still, we would be building a poor user experience, forcing the user to jump through hoops that result in either zero results or the exact same results. At such a low content volume, the best solution would be to simply allow the user to scroll through all of the content.

This shows us that an MVP is not necessarily just a subset of the full set of features: you may instead build a temporary alternative to what you ultimately have planned.

WHAT DOES 'MINIMUM VIABLE PRODUCT' ACTUALLY MEAN?

To wrap up this chapter, let us finish how we probably should have started, by defining the term MVP. In some senses it is pretty self-explanatory, but it will be something slightly different for every startup. Taking the words one at a time:

- Minimum: no more than needed. The thinnest slice of the envisaged ideal that provides value to real-world users and a revenue stream to the startup. Getting the minimum right requires extreme diligence but gets you to market and feedback as quickly as possible, reducing risk.

- Viable: not perfect. Works well enough for the current user base, but may include interim implementations, manual steps, or even known gaps and issues. But from the botanical definition of viable ('able to germinate'), the MVP needs to provide sound footing for frequent future releases and scaling to your expanding user base.

- Product: this is a big one; there is a significant distinction between proof-of-concept and product. Calling something a product confers the weight of customer expectations, and includes all the back-office baggage, boilerplate journeys and accreditation red tape. It is the quality of quality.

The MVP is just the first point on a never-ending roadmap of product development: if you plan it right it will be your version 1.0 release. You will then be free to repeat the process again and again to scope and deliver the next tranche of ideas as quickly and completely as possible.

TAKEAWAYS

- Prioritising for your first release does not mean discarding or devaluing ideas.

- Scope naturally balloons and complexity explodes: minimising scope creep requires a constant effort and vigilance.

- Be realistic about your initial user/data volumes and save time by incorporating tactical and interim solutions into your early releases.

3

TECH VISION AND PRODUCT ROADMAPPING

ALEKSA VUKOTIC

INTRODUCTION

It's important to start small and with a realistic MVP goal, but at the same time we need to know where we are going to ensure that we can support business ambitions, excite investors and challenge the development team. This is where technology vision and the product roadmap come into play. In this chapter, we'll talk about why it is important to be a realist in the short term and an innovator in the long term, and how to get to grips with the fast-paced and changing technology landscape when making long-term decisions.

PRODUCT ROADMAP

The importance of being lean when starting a tech product business (or any business for that matter) cannot be overstated. Unless you have unlimited resources, the only way to prove that your idea and model can be the foundation of a sustainable business is to launch the product and test it in the real world.

That said, it can be dangerous to stay narrowly focused on just your short-term goals all the time. If the initial MVP proves to be a success, your customer will want to see new great features added all the time, and investors will want to see how you can scale the business out from a bedroom-headquartered micro business to a well-oiled tanker navigating to commercial success.

It's not easy to balance these two seemingly opposing goals: launching the MVP in the short term and strategic growth in the long term. Acting small but thinking big is a key ingredient to building a successful business, and in the tech startup world, product roadmaps and technology vision are important tools to achieve this.

THE ROLE OF THE PRODUCT ROADMAP

Let's start with the product roadmap. The product roadmap represents a view of the progress, direction and priorities of the product in the future, including all features and activities. It should be accessible and shared with the entire team, and act as a key document against which everyone can evaluate their contributions. Everything every single team member does, from software developers to sales staff, should be done with the goal of making the future vision in the roadmap a successful reality.

This focus on both the short and long term means that the first section ('near future') of the roadmap should describe the MVP features in clear detail, making a timeline that is ambitious but achievable in three to six months. This first section will have concrete features and activities that are easy to understand and track, and everyone within the company should be able to identify with one or more of the work streams described. It is usually written with a clear timeline plan outlined.

Going beyond the MVP, the roadmap needs to inspire and demonstrate the vision of what else will come in the future. It's hard to predict and prescribe exactly what your product will look like 12 or 18 months from now, or what you'll be able to achieve with your team. There are many challenges ahead, and you may change direction or pivot as a reaction to events, customer feedback and commercial realities. But don't let that stop you: the roadmap is a living document, it will evolve and change as the business grows, and it is expected that you'll need to revisit and update the priorities, both short- and long-term, as you go along.

It's ok to keep the long-term roadmap vague, just describing high-level features rather than the concrete steps of how to deliver them. For example, you could write 'Automate customer payment process' – this doesn't say what exactly you'd do to improve automation, but it makes it clear how you're planning to improve the product: by automating something that is managed as a manual process for now while you're still handling only a few customers.

The product roadmap doesn't have an end. It just describes the road ahead as far as you can see. The closer you get to the future, the more you'll see, and the roadmap should always be updated to reflect that. It's also important to put some signposts into your roadmap: milestones, key dates for reassessment or trade shows, and key resources, for example adding when you're expecting to start hiring for an expanded team to deliver your vision.

ANATOMY OF A PRODUCT ROADMAP

In our view, the product roadmap requires the following characteristics; it should:

- Encompass the entire product: all features and activities you are considering for your product should be included, whether concrete specific features as required by customers, or blue-sky ideas that you have a vision for, or any tech debt, technical or recruitment activities that will affect the product in a significant way.

- Be shared and accessible: everyone in the team should have easy access to the product roadmap and understand where the product is going. This includes key stakeholders and senior management, as well as development, operations and sales teams, and even customers in some cases; everyone you work with and who has a stake in making the product a success.

- Be managed as an evolving document: a product roadmap is never complete. Over time your thinking will most likely change based on external events, customer feedback or technology advancements. It's important to treat the product roadmap as a living document under a regular review process.

- Include a timeline: in order to deliver the promises on the product roadmap, you should define key dates and milestones which you're all working towards. These can correspond to key release dates, marketing activities, conferences or trade shows, or even link to important hires, where additional skills will need to be added in order to execute and deliver particular features. Think of these dates as milestones, not deadlines, used to frame the delivery plan, evaluate investment and resources need, and to communicate what's expected from the team, as well as send key messages to investors and stakeholders about the constant improvement of the company and the product.

The best startups are formed on the ideas and vision championed by the founder or the founding team. Typically this means that the entire product roadmap and vision are within your brain, with you steering product development to match your vision and intuition. But as the product and team grow, this becomes a bottleneck limiting the ability of the startup to scale, so it's best to think about a more formal process to manage the product roadmap.

One of the typical challenges we've seen around this is that the founder doesn't feel they can let go of owning the roadmap on their own, leading to slower product development, lower quality, lack of a common goal within the team, and friction with investors and key stakeholders. To avoid this, you should embrace the fact that as your idea becomes reality and the company grows, you will benefit from a more structured way to manage the product.

Some of the key activities and milestones required in a successful product roadmap management process are listed below:

- Appoint the product owner: someone whose full-time job is to think about the product, constantly validating it, talking to customers and aggregating feedback. The product owner will work closely with the entire team – developers, sales, management, investors – in order to facilitate the creation and review of the product roadmap, and own the communication of the product vision to everyone involved. It can be a part-time role for someone close enough to the product in the early phases, but don't be mistaken and think that it can stay that way. The product owner is a key role within a tech product company, and eventually it should be a full-time responsibility.

- Organise regular product roadmap reviews: at least once a quarter, present the state of the roadmap to the entire team; increase engagement and buy-in from all levels of the organisation by sharing the product vision that everyone is working towards. In addition, use board meetings and other key stakeholder gatherings to present parts of the product roadmap – usually those that are coming next – to maintain excitement and commitment to the product from the board. Finally, ensure you have, at minimum, a monthly product roadmap review so you can gather new ideas and validate current thinking alongside the creative minds within your organisation, as well as ensure that the product roadmap reflects current commercial and technological developments in the industry.

- Align the product roadmap with development and sales/marketing activities: as we said above, the product roadmap needs a timeline and key dates to focus around; ensure that these key dates match the post-engineering capabilities of the team and the marketing plans (events, conferences, etc.) that your sales team are working towards.

What about the tools that should be used to create the roadmap? We've seen great roadmaps maintained in all kinds of ways. The tool itself is not really important, but here are a few ways that you can do it:

- As a spreadsheet: easy to share and access, with familiarity of the spreadsheet software across all parts of the organisation – this is especially true if sales and marketing teams have a lot of input into how the roadmap is developed.

- Jira or other product management software: these typically have decent plugins for managing product roadmaps, so could be a good choice as well. Project management tools have built-in time-tracking capabilities, so adding a timeline and key dates to the roadmap becomes very easy and intuitive. Another added benefit is that, as your development team uses these tools, there is a better chance they'll keep on top of the product roadmap as well.

- Specialist cloud-based tools for product roadmap management (e.g. Roadmunk, Product Plan): these are typically more expensive, but have great features geared towards clear communication of the product vision using the roadmap. This is why these tools are often used to present to the board or wider team, to excite everyone and ensure clear communication of long-term vision.

However, don't focus too much on the tools — instead, ensure that you have a good product roadmap structure and, most importantly, a process that will allow you to develop your founder ideas into the best possible product over time.

TECHNOLOGY VISION

When building a tech business — be it tech product or service offering focused — 'technology vision' is a key element to managing all the technological aspects of the business. Technology vision is about identifying how you need to develop your tech thinking in order to deliver the promises of the roadmap. It covers a number of different elements which we'll explore in the following sections.

PRODUCT ARCHITECTURE

As we will discuss in more detail in Chapter 5, product architecture is important for visualising the system as a whole, identifying the tech components, and communicating your plan for how to build the product to both the software development team and investors and other stakeholders in a clear and concise way.

Due to the nature of lean startups, the architecture needs to be able to evolve all the time, and the technology vision should ideally contain both the MVP architecture illustrating your short-term goals, and a long-term architecture vision illustrating how the system might look in the future if things go according to plan.

TECH STACK: LANGUAGES AND FRAMEWORKS

Programming languages, frameworks and tools are the key ingredients in making a working software product. The product will inherently have characteristics of the tools used to build it, whether that's scalability, readability or maintainability, memory or CPU consumption, performance, etc. It is therefore important to make the right technology choices before starting development.

The technology stack is not only important for its objective characteristics that contribute to the quality of the product; it also plays a key part in enabling motivated and interested team members to solve complex problems. For development teams, it's about enjoying the work, so using the latest technology will go a long way towards ensuring the team work to the best of their abilities.

In addition, the technology recruitment market moves at a similar pace to advancements in technology – very fast! Making sure that the selected technology stack has a deep enough talent pool and online community will make the recruitment and establishment of the team much easier.

You can read more about technology choices and their impact on the tech product in Chapter 7.

INNOVATION AND R&D

Startups are driven by innovation, whether in business models, customer relationships or technology. For any tech-minded startup, ensuring that innovation is at the core of the company should be a key goal, especially during the startup and scaleup stages. That's why it's important to include innovation and research and development (R&D) in your technology vision. R&D ensures that, when developing the product, you're not focused solely on the functional aspects that deliver business value. You should also consider bleeding-edge tech and approaches that may not have a commercial use yet, but could become a big part of the product or company in the future.

Because it's not easy to calculate return on investment for these R&D and innovation activities, it's easy to put them aside when facing pressure from investors or customers. But that is yet another reason why it's important to encourage a culture of innovation within the tech team, to make sure innovation continues.

So how do we do that? There are a number of practices you can foster within your tech team to encourage innovation:

- Create a dedicated R&D time: this is a very efficient way to guarantee free thinking for some of the smartest people you typically employ – the engineering team. Dedicate 10 to 20% of their working week to pure R&D (every Friday for example). Make sure there is minimal structure to this time: allow the team creative freedom to pursue their interests. What you should ensure is a sharing culture: every month, dedicate a day for everyone to share their R&D work and findings; you'll be surprised how many good ideas will find their way into your tech products in this way.

- Encourage blogging: whenever something is achieved of significance outside the company itself (a tech breakthrough, efficiency improvements, etc. – anything that's not part of the business's secret sauce), encourage the team/individuals to write about it and share it on social media. This not only helps develop a personal voice for your engineers, but also gives a tech voice to your company, which will help with attracting talent in the future. One word of caution: writing blogs takes time, so don't expect high-quality blog posts without allowing your team the time to think and write them.

- Conference attendance and speaking: attending and presenting at conferences also ensures the tech voice of the company is heard. This is especially important for startups whose product has a worldwide audience. Ensure there is a budget for conference attendance, it will be money well spent.

- Recruitment for innovation: this can be difficult to achieve, but over time you should focus your hiring strategy on finding talented engineers who are innovators and enjoy R&D, as well as sharing their knowledge with the world.

SECURITY AND PRIVACY

In recent years, the security and privacy of sensitive data has become a hot topic and a priority for customers, governments and regulators. Although the importance of security and privacy depends on the sector and use of the tech product, it is undeniable that they now have a major role to play for most companies and for some sectors in particular.

Take the fintech sector for example: with the open banking and financial API revolution, central banks and regulators have been pushing hard to open the data owned by banking customers to the wider marketplace. As part of the push toward an API-driven ecosystem, the participants have been forced to follow strict guidelines regarding customers' data privacy, security of their financial information and fraud prevention.

The products that are making the most of the situation are those that put security and privacy at the heart of their platforms, making sure that those features are first-class elements of the product. The situation is similar in other sectors: for medtech, for example, it's about protection of the sensitive private information concerning individuals' health.

MOBILE STRATEGY

Mobile channels have become ubiquitous for the modern generation of consumers. With the advent of superfast internet adoption, especially in the mobile sphere with 4G and 5G network development, it has never been easier to access data (and a lot of it) on the move. Whether it's shopping and streaming videos on public transport, paying your bills while in the queue for coffee, using your mobile phone as a companion for daily exercise or learning, or staying in touch with friends, mobile is the key platform for reaching truly global audiences.

It's therefore not surprising that eight out of 10 startups we talk to nowadays are looking to build an app.

The challenge with building an app is that the mobile app and software development ecosystem is very fragmented, making it harder and slower to build quality products, which can therefore make it more expensive (think of the Apple/Android divide; multiple devices and form factors; throw in tablets, and you'll see how quickly it becomes a complex challenge to manage). The skills and talent required for mobile development can be fragmented as well, adding to the complexity of managing the entire process.

It is extremely important to ensure you understand these challenges and develop your mobile strategy so that it works in the short, medium and long term. Some considerations we usually discuss at this stage are:

- **Mobile-friendly web app**: do you definitely need a mobile app? If you have a B2B business model, or the mobile app is planned mainly as a companion to the core desktop/web application, maybe it will be sufficient to have a mobile-friendly version of the main product that runs in a browser and is portable across platforms and devices (of course, this means you won't be able to use any of the native features of the device, such as biometrics and Bluetooth).

- **Progressive web application (PWA)**: the next step up from a mobile-friendly website. It looks like an app, with its own icon, but it's nothing more than a packaged website. It's relatively easy to build if you have a mobile-friendly web product, with the benefit of adding that 'appy' feel to your users. The PWA can be downloaded from your website, so doesn't involve an app store – which is both good (lower barrier to entry, quicker updates) and bad (users can't find it when browsing app store). Although looking like an app, the user experience will be web-like, which is often cited as the main criticism of mobile-friendly or PWA apps, although this needs to be compared with the cost of development and maintenance.

- **Cross-platform app**: the single codebase that complies to mobile apps for all main mobile platforms (Apple and Android mainly). Cross-platform frameworks have grown in popularity recently, as a good balance between single-codebase common code and platform-specific code (for dealing with device hardware like biometrics, camera, phone, etc.). React-native is probably the one with the biggest community at present, therefore our first choice, although Flutter and Xamarine are alternatives. The user experience is much closer to a native app, performance is better than PWA, and you have access to device hardware and the app stores; this makes it a well-balanced approach if using the app stores is a must.

- **Native app**: native apps are developed for the given platform from the ground up. So we have two codebases – one for Android and one for Apple iOS – with separate teams developing and maintaining each, using platform-specific tools and frameworks (Java/Kotlin for Android and ObjectiveC/Swift for iOS). Using native development makes apps more responsive and perform better, and user experience will be the best you can get for any device. But of course this also depends on the quality of the developers building the app, and this is the biggest challenge with native builds. With separate teams and separate code for each platform, it's significantly more expensive to build and maintain the app, and takes longer.

Each product and business model has different requirements, so armed with an understanding of the mobile options, you, the founder, along with your CTO or tech partner, can make the right decision.

CLOUD AND OPERATIONAL CONSIDERATIONS

Chapter 6 is dedicated to cloud computing and its role in startups; however, we'll briefly touch on it here as well due to its importance to the technology vision.

Nothing has democratised access to compute resources like cloud computing: you can now build a world-class infrastructure for a world-class tech product with ease, low initial investment and a cost-effective no-strings-attached commercial model.

Even more importantly, cloud computing goes very much hand in hand with the lean and agile startup mentality: you can start small, with minimal (or even zero) cost, but have the capacity to scale to the level of Google or Facebook if required.

And finally, cloud evolution includes a march toward cloud-managed services, so you can run complex workloads using SQL and NoSQL databases, message queues, containers, and AI and machine learning models using commoditised services without the need for expensive internal infrastructure and skills.

That said, there are many ways a startup can utilise the cloud, and there are trade-offs to be made when choosing between cloud and on-premises infrastructure, typically around offline access, security and privacy, and regulatory environment, depending on where the data are physically stored.

For all these reasons, it's important that your technology vision considers cloud strategy early on, in order to understand the challenges and extract the maximum benefits from this exciting tech sector.

TAKEAWAYS

- The product roadmap formalises product development, motivates all members of the team to work towards the same goal, and improves communication about the product to investors and other stakeholders.

- Keeping all information about the product in the founder's head is not sufficient for the long-term growth of the tech startup – make sure to formalise the product roadmap process, ensure clear ownership and share it with everyone involved using easily-accessible tools.

- Putting in place a process and product owner to oversee the roadmap and product development is key to managing the transition from startup to scaleup.

- Start small but think big – ensure your technology roadmap considers more than just the MVP, including cutting-edge technology that can act as a real differentiator in the future.

- Ensure key technological aspects of your product are thought about early – know your mobile strategy before you invest in building the app; and consider cloud strategy before you need to scale.

4

STARTUP SPRINT

IAN BROOKES

INTRODUCTION

The Startup Sprint© is thestartupfactory.tech methodology for asking and answering critical business questions through design, prototyping, and testing startup venture thinking. It's a structured process to enable founders to focus on their core venture development using best-practice tools in a coherent and integrated approach. It ensures you achieve problem-solution-market fit.

It has the Lean Startup ethos[4] as its core, and layers in the Google Ventures Design Sprint[5] concept. We adopt Steve Blank's customer development process, which feeds into the models developed by the Strategyzer team[6], including value proposition design and the business model canvas.

The process is founded on the agile technique of 'sprints', with fixed working periods having defined outcomes. This enables iteration and pivots in thinking, but also ensures there is an output from the process. It doesn't constrain, rather it guides and ensures we get stuff done – it moves *thinking into doing*.

The outcome is a Venture Vector©, a high-level business strategy and plan that integrates all the thinking for a startup idea, from

---

4 Ries Eric, 6 October 2011, *The Lean Startup: How Constant Innovation Creates Radically Successful Businesses*, Portfolio Penguin

5 Google Ventures, The Design Sprint https://www.gv.com/sprint/

6 Strategyzer: Innovation, strategy, tools and training https://www.strategyzer.com/

the problem to be solved, through user journey mapping, to an informed value proposition design and product feature roadmap, and ultimately an investable business model.

BACKGROUND

The approach takes inspiration from what is surely the greatest ever entrepreneurial journey of all time – Apollo XI putting a man on the moon on 20 July 1969. Let's use this to frame your own startup journey, before highlighting the Startup Sprint© process.

When the lunar module landed at 4.18 pm EDT, astronaut Neil Armstrong radioed: 'Houston, Tranquility Base here. The Eagle has landed.' At 10.56 pm EDT, Armstrong planted the first human foot on the moon. With more than half a billion people watching on television, he climbed down the ladder and proclaimed: 'That's one small step for man, one giant leap for mankind.' Let's make your startup venture journey as spine-tingling as this!

President Kennedy first presented the moon landing proposal to the US public in an address to Congress on 25 May 1961. However, his more famous speech was on 12 September 1962 at Rice University:

> 'We choose to go to the moon in this decade and do the other things, not because they are easy, but because they are hard, because that goal will serve to organise and measure the best of our energies and skills, because that challenge is one that we are willing to accept, one we are unwilling to postpone, and one which we intend to win. We have vowed we will not see space filled with weapons of mass destruction, but with instruments of knowledge and understanding. We intend to be first.'

We want to work with startup founders who share Kennedy's bold ambition to achieve something unique. His goal of putting a man on the moon in less than nine years was a fantastic statement of intent, and the fact that it was done is astounding. Of course, sadly, Kennedy did not live to see his dream realised.

Landing on the moon is surely man's greatest ever entrepreneurial act. Think about it. Go outside tonight and look up. Imagine yourself up there, looking down. *Imagine!* How would you feel, blasting out of the atmosphere, orbiting the Earth, and standing on the moon? WOW!

Courage, ingenuity and one heck of a big adventure, leaping off into the unknown, driven by your vision, just like launching your own startup business. So what can we learn from the extraordinary Apollo XI experience, and how can we put it into our Startup Sprint© process to help your startup?

1) IT STARTS WITH A VISION

'When John Kennedy went before Congress on May 25, 1961 and said we were going to the Moon, our total flight experience was one 15-minute suborbital flight.'

(Dr John Logsdon, Director of the Center for International Science and Technology Policy)

Takeaway: To say Kennedy's vision was bold and set an ambitious timeline is an understatement. As a startup founder, set down your purpose and vision, and have unreasonable expectations that even you don't think are realistic!

2) HAVE A SENSE OF DIRECTION

'We knew what had to be done. How to do it in 10 years was never addressed before the announcement was made. But quite simply, we considered the program a number of phases.'

(Dr Maxime Faget, Chief Engineer and Designer of the Apollo command and lunar modules)[7]

The Apollo programme followed the steps of the Lean Startup, setting a series of milestones: Phase 1 was to fly to the moon, Phase 2 was to orbit the moon, Phase 3 was to land an unmanned craft on the moon, and so on. They followed the concept of 'the pivot', from the Lean Startup. Had they immediately set their sights on a full-fledged lunar landing, history may have turned out very differently.

Takeaway: When launching your startup, there are unknown unknowns, so don't bother trying to craft a detailed plan based on guesses; instead, break it down into the major steps and focus on attaining each one, one at a time.

3) A STARTUP IS AN EXPERIMENT

'We said to ourselves that we have now done everything we know how to do. We feel comfortable with all of the unknowns that we went into this program with. We don't know what else to do to make this thing risk-free, so it's time to go.'

(Dr Christopher Kraft, Director of Flight Operations)[8]

The Apollo XI mission was one of the most risky undertakings in human history. From technical failure to human error, any number of things could have gone wrong, and did. NASA handled risk by actively

---

7 NASA, Managing the Moon Program: Lessons Learned From Project Apollo, Proceedings of an Oral History Workshop conducted 21 July 1989 https://history.nasa.gov/monograph14.pdf

8 NASA, Managing the Moon Program: Lessons Learned From Project Apollo, Proceedings of an Oral History Workshop conducted 21 July 1989 https://history.nasa.gov/monograph14.pdf

looking for it and constantly asking themselves, *What if?* Without taking those risks, the achievement would never have been accomplished.

Takeaway: As with any experiment, a startup is about setting down hunches and testing them. The build-measure-learn approach is one of the Lean Start-up's key principles that we include in the Startup Sprint©. It's about calculated risks: don't let an acceptable amount of risk keep you from pushing ahead.

4) ITERATE, AND DON'T BE AFRAID TO MODIFY THE PLAN

'They probably normally expected us to land with about two minutes of fuel left. And here we were, still a hundred feet above the surface, at 60 seconds.'

(Buzz Aldrin, Lunar Module Pilot)[9]

On the descent to the moon, the lunar module's computer became overloaded with data, threatening to reboot in the middle of the landing sequence. Aldrin discovered they were going to miss their target, and would likely smash into a crater at an alarming velocity. Armstrong took manual control, while Aldrin fed him altitude and velocity data. They successfully landed on the moon's surface with just seconds of fuel left. If Armstrong and Aldrin hadn't acted fast, Armstrong's iconic moonwalk would never have happened.

Takeaway: No business plan survives first contact with a customer, so remember that even the most well-thought-out startup plans may need to be altered if circumstances change or a new opportunity arises.

9 Highfield Roger, (2019), 'Apollo 11 Moon Landing: The Most Difficult Moments', 20 July 2019, available at: https://blog.sciencemuseum.org.uk/apollo-11-moon-landing-the-most-difficult-moments/

5) KEEP ASKING QUESTIONS AND LEARNING

'When we had the Apollo I fire, we took a step back and asked what lessons have we learned from this horrible tragedy? Now let's be doubly sure that we are going to do it right the next time.'

(Dr Christopher Kraft, Director of Flight Operations)[10]

The Apollo programme was home to some of the world's most brilliant minds, and no one was shy about their mistakes. They made recording and learning from their errors a central part of their process. Failure was simply an opportunity to learn and improve.

According to NASA, every successful project needs three things: a vision, a vivid picture of where you're going; complete commitment from leadership to make it happen; and a first goal to keep everyone focused based on learning. The Lean Startup philosophy adopts this too: the first version of your 'thing', the minimum viable product (MVP), is based on validated learning.

Takeaway: For a startup, get out of the building, talk to prospective customers and fail fast – validated learning and making retrospectives an ongoing part of your project are vital, not one-time events; they are crucial to startup success.

THE STARTUP SPRINT©

Apollo XI saw NASA invest a decade into training and preparation, absorbing the setbacks as well as keeping the dream alive. Life has its twists and turns – Armstrong was nearly killed twice in his NASA

---

10 NASA, Managing the Moon Program: Lessons Learned From Project Apollo, Proceedings of an Oral History Workshop conducted 21 July 1989 https://history.nasa.gov/monograph14.pdf

training, but he never quit. Success is failure turned inside out, and you never can tell quite how close you are.

Apollo XI captured the true spirit of pioneering entrepreneurship, and Steve Blank, a colleague of Eric Ries in the Lean Startup movement, has rewritten Kennedy's Apollo vision, capturing Armstrong's spirit:

> 'We choose to invest in ideas, not because they are easy, but because they are hard, because that goal will serve to organise and measure the best of our energies and skills, because that challenge is one that we are willing to accept, one we are unwilling to postpone, and one which we intend to win.'[11]

That's the spirit we've baked into the Startup Sprint©. Here's a summary of the approach; the tools we apply in our programme.

SPRINT 1: MOONSHOT: WHAT'S THE BIG HAIRY AUDACIOUS GOAL?

This sprint is about shaping your thinking underpinning your proposed venture, applying the Lean Startup approach and other leading startup planning techniques to shape a prototype, and identifying the aspects of your proposed venture that you want to know more about or validate.

You'll get valuable feedback to assess what you don't know and what you need to figure out next. From this, you'll start to design the experiments to undertake a customer discovery process to learn about your customer and validate your assumptions.

11 Blank Steve, (2012), 'Why Facebook Is Killing Silicon Valley', 21 May 2012, available at: https://steveblank.com/2012/05/

- Tools: visioning; Lean Startup; peer presentations.

- Outcomes: Lean Startup outputs; customer discovery plan (personas, assumptions, scenarios).

SPRINT 2: DESIGNING YOUR ROCKET: WHAT DOES A CUSTOMER LOOK LIKE?

Sprint two adopts elements of the Google Ventures Design Sprint to shape your problem-solution thinking from a customer's perspective, followed by using the customer development framework developed by Steve Blank to test underlying assumptions.

The call to action is 'get out of the building' to test face to face with target/potential users and customers. This helps to rule in and out all sorts of early-stage thinking and focus on the aspects of your innovation that provide customer value.

- Tools: design sprint thinking; customer discovery experiments (Steve Blank); user story and prototyping; peer presentations.

- Outcomes: customer maps; user story mapping; product prototype designs.

SPRINT 3: LET'S BUILD A ROCKET: WHAT'S YOUR VALUE PROPOSITION?

We apply the Strategyzer Value Proposition Canvas as a process and a tool to collate the customer discovery feedback, and ask the question, 'Pivot or persevere?' You'll evolve your point of view on the offering your venture aims to provide based on the feedback gained and validated learning.

From this, we'll build a feature set and development plan for the envisaged value proposition into a product roadmap. We use case studies of how other organisations have developed their innovations – the iPhone is a great case study.

- Tools: value proposition canvas; product roadmaps; case studies; peer presentations.

- Outcomes: value proposition; product roadmap.

SPRINT 4: HOW TO LAUNCH A ROCKET: WHAT'S YOUR BUSINESS MODEL?

The process and outcome for sprint four adopts the Strategyzer Business Model Canvas tool – now you have an informed understanding of what your customers want, how are you going to get a venture launched to make it happen, and be a success?

We look at examples of successful innovative business models – Tesla, Uber and Apple – which have both innovation and customers at the core of their offerings, to keep pushing your thinking. This will include developing your go-to-market strategy: a launch plan to find, win and keep customers.

- Tools: business model canvas; case studies; find-win-keep customer mapping.

- Outcomes: business models; launch plan; customer acquisition plans.

SPRINT 5: GO! CAN YOU MAKE IT HAPPEN?

This is it! It's time to decide whether you have a venture worth launching with the ambition to scale up. You can't do it all on your own, you need resources – primarily a team and finances – and we will help you build these key elements into your business launch plan.

We bring everything together using our Venture Vector© process and tool, a high-level business strategy and plan that integrates the outcomes from the first four sprints into a single, coherent *Go!* plan.

- Tools: Venture Vector©; case studies and guest founder presentations; financial model.

- Outcomes: Venture Vector© business strategy and plan; financial model; investor pitch.

CONCLUSION

The Apollo XI mission is, to me, the ultimate startup and best example of launching a large-scale high-risk technology project to achieve something no one has done before. It resonates with Simon Sinek's work on *Why?*[12] in terms of having a clear vision and purpose underpinning your startup ambition.

It was about turning an idea into reality, an example of what Steve Jobs termed 'the reality distortion field'. Ignore the naysayers, it can be done. 'We can lick gravity, but sometimes paperwork is overwhelming', said Wernher von Braun, Chief Architect of Apollo's Saturn V launch rocket, capturing the spirit of adventure.[13]

'Only those who will risk going too far can possibly find out how far one can go', said T.S. Eliot.[14] Eric Ries defines a startup as 'a human

12 Sinek Simon, 6 October 2011, *Start With Why: How Great Leaders Inspire Everyone To Take Action*, Penguin

13 NASA, Managing the Moon Program: Lessons Learned From Project Apollo, Proceedings of an Oral History Workshop conducted 21 July 1989 https://history.nasa.gov/monograph14.pdf

14 Eliot T.S. 1931, *Preface to Transit of Venus (Poems by Harry Crosby)*

institution designed to deliver a new product or service under conditions of extreme uncertainty'[15]. Everything about NASA, the 2,500 who worked on the Apollo XI project, and the astronauts – Armstrong, Aldrin and Collins – makes them startup founders and entrepreneurs. What a leap for mankind they made. Now make one for yourself.

TAKEAWAYS

- Set down your purpose and vision; have unreasonable expectations that even you don't think are realistic!

- When launching your startup, there are unknown unknowns, so don't bother trying to craft a detailed plan based on guesses; instead, break it down into the major steps and focus on attaining each one, one at a time.

- A startup is about testing your hunches. Take calculated risks; don't let an acceptable amount of risk keep you from pushing ahead.

- Remember that even the most well-thought-out startup plans may need to be altered if circumstances change or a new opportunity arises.

- Get out of the building, talk to prospective customers and fail fast – validated learning should be an ongoing part of your process.

- By using the Startup Sprint© you will gradually build a high-level business strategy and plan for your startup.

15 Ries Eric, 6 October 2011, *The Lean Startup: How Constant Innovation Creates Radically Successful Businesses*, Portfolio Penguin

5

SOFTWARE ARCHITECTURE

ALEKSA VUKOTIC

INTRODUCTION

The topic of software architecture is often discussed when we consider thoroughly thought-out software builds. The idea that, to build quality and functional software, we need to think about overall structure and design, just as architects do when designing a building, seems to be common sense.

However, the need for upfront work or decisions often clashes with the startup mantra of moving fast and failing fast until you find the winning formula. Indeed, startups often don't know what kind of business model they will end up using, and may well have to change direction many times while trying to keep afloat, so does it make sense to invest in robust software architecture and design at an early stage?

Taking a very agile approach to building software in a startup often results in a hacky solution, without structure or design. This approach can certainly deliver a software product quickly, but any evolution of such a software product – changing its functionality and scope, growing the team or scaling the business – becomes increasingly difficult.

In the following sections, we'll discuss some of these challenges and try to find a balanced path that works in a fast-paced startup environment, while ensuring that enough architectural thinking is baked in from the early stages.

IMPORTANCE OF SOFTWARE ARCHITECTURE

Before digging deeper into some concrete architectural concepts, let's discuss why software architecture is important for successful project delivery.

BETTER UNDERSTANDING OF THE SYSTEM

The first goal of software architecture is to be able to identify all the interacting components of a system, including individual parts that may work independently but contribute to the system as a whole. As an example, a typical system will have some form of front-end channel/component (web portal or mobile app), a backend (handling all the heavy lifting) and a database (for long-term, durable data storage).

If you take one step deeper, backend usually contains a number of components (API, processing service, notifications service, etc.); being able to describe and refer to each individual component makes it much easier to explain and communicate the software design and bridge the communications gap between technical (development teams) and functional (founder and customer) perspectives.

ESTIMATION AND COST MANAGEMENT

Estimating the effort required to build anything is a hard task, and the nature of software development makes this even more difficult. Why? Software is an effort of the mind, problem-solving in real time. Although there are many patterns and open source libraries that solve a lot of common problems, composing those into a functional and high-performance system is not done in a factory-manufactured way, but rather is crafted using the individual skills of developers.

In addition, software and hardware are complex beasts; a lot of unexpected and unknown things can happen during the development process. And there is a communications gap between founders and marketeers, with their functional mindset, and the techies who are often thinking on a more in-depth, technical level.

Simplifying a complex system by visualising its interacting components makes it much easier to understand and describe, and also splits the problem into smaller pieces, allowing a more accurate estimation of the effort required to build it.

EFFICIENT SCALABILITY

When we mention scalability, we often think of horizontal scalability of software systems – the ability of the tech product to handle ever more and more customers/requests by simply adding extra commodity-grade hardware. This is important for any growing business: the last thing we want as a founder, after all our hard work on functionality and marketing, is for the system to collapse when we're on the cusp of going big.

In order to have a scalable system, the relevant properties need to be thought of and built in from the start, and are closely related to overall architectural decisions, starting with data models and a database engine, followed by service boundaries and communication protocols, and including front-end as well.

Scaling data

For example, selecting a database and data model has significant consequences for scalability. The typical (and, until a few years back, standard) choice would be an SQL database such as MySQL – open source, easy to manage, with a large online community, what's not to like? And indeed, MySQL is a good choice for many tech products.

However, if you're planning to be able to support millions of concurrent users, à la Google scale (maybe you're building a new ubiquitous social network or a streaming service), SQL databases can quickly become a bottleneck given the way they store data in a tabular format, specifically if you need to join many tables to get aggregate data sets.

Since the trend towards massive scale began (with Google, Amazon, Facebook and the like), this problem has been solved many times, so we now have a large and growing number of NoSQL databases, named as such to illustrate their opposing characteristics to traditional SQL.

They promise massive scale, easy horizontal scaling by adding new instances with a button click, and ingenious data modelling techniques using semi-structured or connected data models. However, there's one thing to remember: all this comes at a cost in terms of database functionality, based on characteristics of the distributed data system.

The three main characteristics of distributed data systems are:

- **Consistency**: ensuring that once the data is written, any part of the system will be guaranteed to see the new data immediately.

- **Availability**: ability to respond under any load – a key property of scalable systems.

- **Partition tolerance**: ability to serve ALL the data, even if big chunks of the system become disconnected.

It's a hard truth that any distributed system can only have at most TWO of these – never all three. SQL databases offer consistency (with their ACID transaction support) and typically one of the other two properties (see CAP theorem: https://en.wikipedia.org/wiki/CAP_theorem). NoSQL databases typically sacrifice consistency (often in the form of eventual consistency or tunable consistency) to enable massive scalability.

This sounds reasonable – trade-off one feature for something else that's more important to our use case. But it goes the other way as well: if your startup is a financial institution that relies on transactional data storage (you can't take money from one account and not be sure whether it's visible to everyone or not), consistency becomes a key characteristic, making SQL databases possibly a better choice (we are slightly simplifying the argument here, so be sure that your tech team understand the challenges and choices they face).

Scaling services

Typical software systems have a few defined layers to make them easy to talk about – front-end, backend and database, for example. Backend, or services as we like to call it, is the brains of the system; this is where all the smart stuff happens, devised by you, the founder, and implemented by your geeky but extremely smart dev team.

Databases typically contain state, making them the hardest to scale well. One takeaway here is that anything that has state is hard to scale. As an example, imagine that you store your user's session on the backend side – if the user executes another action, we'll have to make sure that we take into account their session, meaning that we have to either share that session across all backend servers or share the session between them (so it becomes a database problem).

By far the best way to ensure scalable services is to avoid state in this layer, which is called **stateless architectures**. If your backend is stateless, in order to scale it, all we have to do is add more servers (this is called horizontal scaling). We put a load balancer in front of them (which simply distributes user requests across all servers equally), and we have a scalable system. Any request, from any user or any country, can be handled by ANY backend server. If we get more load, we simply add more servers. If any of the servers fail, we replace them. Sounds good, doesn't it?

There are many different ways to actually design such systems, and we'll touch on microservices architectures and reactive systems a bit later.

You may ask: what about vertical scaling? In contrast to horizontal scaling (where we add commodity-grade hardware to improve the system as a whole), vertical scaling is a technique where we keep that first single server, but beef it up by adding more resources – more CPU, memory, disk… It's a valid strategy in some use cases (especially for CPU-intensive problems). However, it does have the flaw that it's much less resilient: if your great big server dies, the entire system goes down with it.

Scaling teams

When talking about scalability, we often assume we're talking about system properties (databases, services, software, hardware); however, equally – if not more – important is the ability to scale the teams.

Solving any problem, however complex or big, is easier if we can split it and solve pieces of it in parallel. In software development, that means having multiple team members (or even multiple teams) delivering individual parts of the system that combine into a whole.

To be able to work on parallel work streams, the system components need to be well defined and clearly understood so that individual developers can work on separate parts, confident that what they are building will be one well-oiled cog in a large machine.

This is one of the things software architecture can best help with: defining components and their interactions so that they can be built and delivered more efficiently and in parallel.

Now this may not be a problem founders recognise at the beginning – after all, you can barely pay that one junior developer that is building the MVP as it is – and that's ok. However, always try to see the bigger picture. If that big breakthrough happens, and you are suddenly under pressure to deliver much more in a short period of time, you need to be able to scale your dev team so that they can continue to be productive.

FUNCTIONAL AGILITY

Let's imagine a situation: we have been building our tech product and everything is going fine. Then, one month before the release, a big competitor launches a product that makes a lot of our features obsolete. What do we do? Most founders find themselves in a similar situation to this at some point; they re-group, re-evaluate and pivot their business model, finding a creative way to ensure the business still adds value and that customers are excited and willing to pay for that value.

Brilliant, so we have an idea how to pivot, and all that's left is to repurpose the product we're already building for the new goal! However, this is where problems often start: in order to make the required changes to the tech, we're told we need to rewrite big chunks of the system, meaning that a lot of the time and resources that have already been spent will go to waste. Situations like this can break a startup.

This is where functional agility in software design and architecture comes into play. When designing a system, especially in a startup environment, it's critical to take **extensibility** into consideration. It's not IF we ever pivot, it's HOW we proceed WHEN we pivot. This means making systems easy to extend and adapt to any new reality, using reusable and generic components and services that are adaptable when change is required.

Although often not considered or forgotten, in our view this is one of the key values of good startup software architecture: the ability to change focus or pivot a product along with the business, with minimal waste.

ARCHITECTURAL CONCEPTS YOU SHOULD KNOW ABOUT

So far we have discussed why, as a startup founder, you should care about software architecture and some of the key concepts and considerations that come with that. Let's take a bit of a deeper dive now into a few architectural concepts you may have heard of which are key within the software industry.

CLOUD-NATIVE ARCHITECTURE

Since its arrival on the scene, cloud computing has become a common topic of conversation within both technology and business circles. In short, cloud computing has resulted in a paradigm shift in how we think about compute resources, making compute power an on-demand commodity, managed in a way so that it doesn't require much direct involvement from the user.

Cloud computing covers every aspect of processing infrastructure we're familiar with: hardware, CPU and memory processing power, durable disk storage and network infrastructure (infrastructure-as-a-service, or IaaS), as well as highly abstracted managed platform-services like SQL and NoSQL databases, message bus and container orchestration systems (platform-as-a-service, or PaaS).

To complete this buzzword bingo, let's add another one: software-as-a-service (SaaS). As a tech business, this is the smart, value-adding product you want to build, based on your ideas and knowledge of the market and customer needs. Any business should strive to build great tech products, and using existing technologies and platforms to help them get there is the shortest and most cost-efficient way. In other words, look to use IaaS and PaaS in order to deliver your best ever SaaS product! (That was a lot of abbreviation!)

When it comes to architecture, the traditional way of moving a tech product or system to the cloud involves basically transforming and migrating your existing, on-premises infrastructure and platforms into the cloud. While there are established processes to achieve this, it's not always a trivial task. Not only do some custom-made on-premises platforms not have ready-made cloud counterparts, even those that do require a completely different mindset and a significant change in management and security practices.

The more modern solution is cloud-native architecture, which means ensuring from the inception that your design and architecture follows all cloud best practices, so that you can use the best features of cloud computing and enable seamless scaling and full automation of technology development and operational elements.

Cloud-native architecture isn't just using the cloud, but making cloud features (IaaS and PaaS) key components in the overall system design, from virtual machines and networking to scalable containers and microservices, managed databases and message bus for rapid development and efficient operational maintenance, all the way to how we manage security, access control and privacy, share data and APIs, and adapt to changes in scalability requirements and technological advancements.

POWER OF APIS

API (application programming interface) is a standardised, machine-understandable language used to enable communication between applications without human interaction.

When a human interacts with a computer or piece of software, we're using human-accessible interfaces to do so: a screen, keyboard and mouse, touchscreen or voice. How about when computers and software communicate among themselves? This is where APIs come into play. Just as a touchscreen allows humans to issue commands and receive information from the machine, the machines can use an interface tailored to their needs to achieve the same goals.

Why is this important? We have all witnessed the uniqueness of the internet in modern society; everything and everyone is connected via this world wide web. The current trend in massive connectivity is the 'Internet of Things', where the devices we use in our daily lives, no matter how large or small, are connected – think of wearables, smart speakers, light switches, gas meters, smart fridges or cars.

These devices use the internet to access and share data between themselves or some centralised systems. All these devices need to be managed remotely. And most of them don't have touchscreens or keyboards to interact with. The only way you can build a system that can consistently communicate with a wide array of devices, send and receive data, remotely manage hardware and software, and ensure security and privacy concerns are addressed is by using a language that all machines can speak. That is what APIs give us.

API-centric architecture allows us to benefit from massive inter-connectivity in a number of ways:

- Specialised services: APIs give the ability to design and build specialised services that do one thing particularly well, and expose them internally and externally for wider usage (a first step towards microservices architectures).

- A collaborative approach: this allows multiple services (built by multiple teams) to communicate with each other to create a richer user journey or a feature larger than the sum of all parts.

- Flexibility: this means functionality can be repurposed or evolved by simply employing APIs in a different way.

- Automation and scalability: using APIs we can build and compose software that is made with a minimum amount of human management in mind, promoting automation and scalability within the tech product.

- Commoditise algorithms and data: businesses whose biggest value is data, need new and innovative ways to monetise that data; API flexibility provides the most efficient way to share that data with your clients and customers.

- Extend customer reach or value: using APIs, your product does not have to be limited to a single customer channel (a mobile app for example); others can be embedded into different customer-facing channels, fostering, for example, B2B collaboration and partnerships at the same time.

Building an API-enabled ecosystem requires planning ahead to ensure that the product architecture allows for the addition of APIs now or in the future. Think about how you can use APIs to empower your product, and then talk to your tech team about the API-specific components you'll need, for example an authorisation server, API gateway or developer portal.

REACTIVE SYSTEMS

Traditionally, software systems have been designed and built to minimise failure, with extensive testing, heavy-handed process to production releases, detailed monitoring and alerting, etc. And while you can certainly minimise the number and impact of failures by proactively monitoring the system, it is a hard reality that failures do still happen, often when you least expect or need them, and can impact the business significantly, be it via missed sales or reputational impact.

Hardware can be unreliable, networks can be flaky, software can have bugs: all of these are hard truths, no matter the innovation in the field or how good the established processes are.

So what is the traditional approach when failure is detected in the system? It varies from organisation to organisation, but the process usually involves incident management calls which include personnel ranging from developers and ops/dev-ops to product owners and customer service representatives trying to:

1. Put in place short-term fixes, while firefighting the problem to return the system to normal service as quickly as possible.

2. Understand the root cause of the failure so it can be addressed and future incidents prevented; it is important to have a robust process for dealing with failure, but it's expensive and time-consuming.

The firefighting part is clearly important: there is not much point trying to repair houses or build new ones while 'London is still burning'. However, understanding the root cause and how to prevent similar problems in the future is significantly more important (hands up anyone who has been involved with firefighting the same issue more than once? More than twice? Exactly).

The usual scenario is that firefighting takes up most of the time of anyone involved in it on the day, so there is less time and concentration to do the all-important root cause analysis and future prevention without markedly increasing the cost of the whole exercise. Is there a better way to approach system failure situations? How about if we designed our system in such a way that it does the firefighting bit on its own, independently and without our help? This would allow the team to focus solely on the root cause analysis and prevention.

Then there is another type of production failure that is relatively frequent: failure of external systems. It's not just our products that suffer from the universal truth that hardware and software failures are inevitable – every other system we interact with is as well. Even Google's services fail occasionally (rarely, but very visibly if you follow any kind of social media). And here is another truth: we can't do much about it. If our systems depend on an external one, failure of the external system will invariably affect ours, and there is no way to proactively avoid it.

However, there is something we can do. We can design our systems in such a way that they can handle failures on their own. When an external service fails, we have the full expectation that parts of our product which depend on it will have degraded functionality, and we let our customers know what's happening. Then, when an external service incident is resolved (you can expect Google to be quick at it, other providers maybe less so), our systems should spring back to life as if nothing happened, importantly without any manual intervention.

Development best practices and dev-ops techniques go a long way towards making failure detection and recovery efficient. We won't discuss these in detail here; instead, I'd like to explore how system design can help us to handle failures in various scenarios like the two described above, with the use of **reactive systems**.

The ideas underpinning reactive systems design have been around for a while, but have gained traction recently with the popularity of microservices architectures, containers and cloud infrastructure. As described in the reactive manifesto (www.reactivemanifesto. org), reactive means **responsive, resilient, elastic** and **message-driven**. Let's think how each of these characteristics affects the failure scenarios we described above, thinking about design of the system as a whole:

- Responsive: a responsive system will give a response to the user even under duress; if any user request cannot be served, it will still let the user know, without potentially exhausting resources that would bring the entire system to a halt. For the scenarios above, this would minimise the number of firefighting incidents; the system will never be completely unusable, so we can concentrate our efforts on the parts of it exposed to failure.

- Resilient: systems should be resilient to failure as much as possible; failure of one part should not impact other components, and in case of external failure the system should be able to self-heal. Think of the compartmentalisation of large ships: in case of hull breach, each of the compartments will fill with water. But because the compartments are separate, water won't fill the entire ship, and the ship can continue to sail until at least the next port or destination.

- Elastic: it should be possible to increase (or decrease) the capacity of a modern software system by changing the number of deployed services. The reactive system will go one step further and react to changes in load automatically, by adding or removing resources as required. If you expect a higher load on your system at a certain time (think the last day of the month for payments, or tax submission deadline day), by making the system elastic and able to increase its resources – whether that's threads, processes or even machines – you can avoid failures due to increased demand.

- Message-driven: to be truly reactive, systems should allow location and time transparency by communicating asynchronously via message-passing. There are many nice features that come from fully async systems – no cascading of failures, natural load balancing due to location transparency, easy flow control using backpressure. In many ways, the message-driven nature of reactive systems complements all of its other key characteristics: responsiveness, resilience and elasticity.

These ideas are not new, but are important in order to build a scalable computer system, and are even more important in the technology startup world where businesses usually start small but can easily grow big, as large as the world wide web can allow. Being able to start nimble but use the same system design to easily grow and scale is a great feature to have.

TAKEAWAYS

- Think about architecture as a set of clear and simple blueprints that your engineering team can use to build a stable and long-lasting system.

- Even if you're not a techie, ensure you understand the key architectural characteristics of your tech product.

- Common understanding of the system, helping engineering teams work toward the same goal, is important for sharing knowledge within the growing team and ensuring good internal understanding of the product.

- Scalability and resilience of the system are directly related to the way it's designed and architected.

6

CLOUD TECH 101

ALEKSA VUKOTIC

INTRODUCTION

Cloud has changed how we think about computing: it has helped us access on-demand infrastructure and platform resources, and outsource tasks that in the past required highly paid specialist resources, such as database management, monitoring and security. In this chapter, we look at how to compare and select cloud providers, which cloud services you should use and how to create cloud-native digital tech products from scratch.

HOW CLOUD CHANGED EVERYTHING

Traditionally, building technology products consisted of two phases: designing and developing the software, and engineering and configuring the hardware where it would run. There was an interdependence between the two, where the software needed to be designed for the particular platform in mind, and infrastructure teams needed to know the inner workings of the software that was to be deployed.

The drawbacks of such an approach quickly become apparent:

- The big initial capital cost: putting together an infrastructure that can not only be used on initial release, but can also be scaled for the as-yet-unproven business plan and forecasts, results in hardware costs often exceeding the cost of building software.

- Inflexible scaling: it is hard to scale should your product be more successful than expected, but will also result in a lot of waste if the user base doesn't grow as expected, with limited ability to scale down hardware resources.

- Inefficient skills distribution: with the required but limited knowledge of infrastructure for the development team, and required but limited knowledge of software for the operations team, software and hardware setup is often inefficient, hard to maintain and has a lot of grey areas around who is responsible for what within the teams.

- Large variety of skills required: in order to build and launch a tech product offering, the team needs not only software developers, but also database administrators, messaging and networking experts, and security personnel. The bigger the team, the more difficult it becomes to organise and streamline teamwork, resulting in delays, bottlenecks and time waste.

Even though most of these drawbacks were known for a long time, there was nothing much that could be done to improve things. Larger companies could build a specialised 'service' team that supported multiple products (e.g. DBA team, networking team), making a first, albeit basic, managed-service offering, where developers could then rely on someone else to take care of the other more standard parts of the software product. However, once cloud computing came on the scene, it was clear that this was a solution that could change the landscape as we knew it. It brought:

- On-demand infrastructure, easy to scale up and down, responding to demand and managing costs early on in the product life cycle.

- Managed standard services, such as databases, message queues, data analytics etc., provisioned on demand and scalable to millions of users/requests.

- One-click standardised security and access-control.

Most IT companies and departments saw the value of such an approach, which is one of the reasons cloud computing has exploded in the last decade and become the de facto standard, from early-stage startups to the highly regulated financial and medical industries.

The ability to start small and scale as required has resonated specifically with startups, aligning with the lean startup minimal waste mantra. It has been cloud computing that has democratised access to world-class infrastructure for all, promoting innovation and research on a scale never seen before.

To understand how cloud computing can influence how you develop a tech product, let's start by having a look at the main cloud providers you could use.

WHICH CLOUD PROVIDER?

Several years back, a lot of stock market pundits were caught by surprise when the Amazon conglomerate started to be profitable much earlier than expected, driven by the growth of Amazon Web Services (AWS), their cloud computing department. To anyone familiar with the trends in the IT industry, this hasn't been a surprise, with AWS being an early leader in the up-and-coming cloud space. AWS has been a pioneer and a long-time leader in the sector; easy provisioning of EC2 instances (Amazon's virtual machines), Amazon Machine Images (AMIs) provided easy infrastructure provisioning and S3 Object Storage, and DynamoDB provided the first data store as a service on a massive scale.

Once it became apparent that the cloud was here to stay, other leading internet companies started making up for lost time, so that nowadays there is not a huge difference between offerings and costs.

Virtual machines and core networking offerings are converging among providers, as well as standard object storage and database-as-a-service offerings. The main competition is based on advanced service offerings, e.g. AI and machine learning, for which the standards are still developing.

- **AWS** is still the market leader, with an ever-expanding array of services. Its S3 Object storage is now used not only by millions of users and companies worldwide, but also by other cloud providers which have built their object storage offering on top of it. In terms of access control and security configuration flexibility, AWS is still among the best options, with IAM roles (although complex) catering for even the trickiest use cases. Database as a service offering has been extended from DynamoDB to support RDS (relational database service), so you can use any major SQL database as a service. In addition, AWS includes some of the more popular NoSQL solutions (DynamoDB, DocumentDB, Mongo Compatible, etc.).

- **Microsoft Azure** entered the cloud space early, but has lagged behind AWS in terms of functionality and cost-effectiveness. Geared towards the larger corporate sector with legacy Microsoft services, it made the cloud transition for such companies easier. For example, Azure offers Active Directory that seamlessly extends or integrates with existing on-premise out-of-the-box solutions. That said, Azure has gone a long way in the last few years to bridge the gap with AWS: usability, automation capabilities and a push for standardisation (in container orchestration space and kubernetes) have raised Azure to be on par with, if not ahead of, competitors in some of these offerings. It supports main SQL and NoSQL databases as a service, and has object storage capability, although that is not yet on the level of AWS S3. Costs were the area where AWS had a clear advantage for a long time; however, this too has changed – now you can expect Azure to be only ever so slightly more expensive overall.

- **Google Cloud Platform** is the search giant's offering in the cloud space. Although known as the pioneers of web-scale software, Google has long used its capabilities and know-how internally, and only started to focus more on usability and public cloud offerings in the last few years. However, Google being Google, it has quickly become one of the leading public cloud platforms available. The fact that Google uses its cloud capability to power vast arrays of internal services has allowed it to offer the spare capacity at competitive prices. In terms of service offering, GCP has taken a different strategy to its main competitors: instead of supporting open source and commercial software in cloud environments, it pushed its own comparable products. So, where AWS and Azure offer Mysql and PostgreSQL relational databases, in GCP you have CloudSQL. The NoSQL offering is based on Google's own BigTable and Firebase databases. This means anyone using these services on GCP is more locked into the ecosystem, making it harder to migrate away. Finally, due to Google owning and developing Android mobile OS, GCP has close integration with services that aid mobile development for Android, such as the Firebase suite of services (more on this in the final section of this chapter).

- **Digital Ocean** is a new entrant in the cloud provider market. What it lacks in services and functionality, it makes up for in ease of use, as well as more-than-competitive pricing. Digital Ocean only supports a few managed databases, has a simpler networking and security model, and doesn't support much integration with enterprise software. However, it's a real joy to use, and nowhere else can you get a 2GB VM (a 'Droplet' in Digital Ocean speak) for a mere $15 per month. It's definitely worth looking at for early startup products or POC/MVP offerings.

- **IBM Cloud** and **Oracle Cloud** are two other providers that have developed quickly in the last few years. Similar to Azure, they are geared towards complex corporate requirements and hybrid deployment with on-premises and private data centres, especially in companies already using a lot of IBM or Oracle services. IBM also has Watson, its well-known cloud AI system. Oracle, on the other hand, provides access to bare metal CPU resources, with the per-CPU power of Oracle virtual machines being an order of magnitude faster and more powerful than some of the standard virtualised CPU offerings from competitors. While both IBM and Oracle are reasonably good choices, due to their lack of focus on smaller use-cases and public offerings, less mature automation and usability, we'd only look at them in specific scenarios (e.g. if you're building B2B software and your main customers are large corporates).

The choice of cloud provider used to be more important in the early days of cloud computing. With the market clearly moving towards cloud as a mainstream for deploying workloads, most leading players have converged to a mature offering, and with a number of agile new entrants, it's never been a better time to enter the cloud arena.

Your first criterion when choosing a cloud provider should be functionality: if you're looking to take advantage of Android and Firebase integration, GCP may be the way to go; if you need active directory or are using Windows and Microsoft Tech Stack, Azure may be a good choice; for cutting-edge server-less technology or a wide array of cloud-based services, AWS may be a good option; if you're looking to sell into large corporates already using IBM or Oracle software, check out IBM Cloud or Oracle Cloud.

The second criterion has to be cost, and you should look at the overall cost here, not just the headline per-hour or estimated monthly cost of cloud infrastructure. What we mean by overall cost is the time and effort needed to set up and configure the cloud, and for ongoing maintenance and operational overheads (monitoring and alerting), on top of the financial cost.

Look at its automation capabilities, documentation, support and online communities and talent pool interested in this cloud. When it comes to headline cost, with good automation capabilities and available documentation, Digital Ocean is definitely worth a look. On pure automation capabilities, AWS is still the market leader, although GCP and Azure are quickly catching up.

Let's now take a look at some of the concrete services you may want to consider when developing your cloud strategy.

CLOUD SERVICES YOU SHOULD KNOW ABOUT

CONTAINER ORCHESTRATION

The rise of containers has had a major influence on how we design and build scalable platforms. How do we best describe containers? Let's first understand how the backend software has been packaged and distributed so far. In the past, the standard way of packaging applications and services was in the form of platform-specific binaries. Think of the installer package for any software you use: before you download it, you need to select a package specific to your hardware or operating system. Similarly, in a software services world, you'd have to build your binaries for the target system you use, e.g. Intel or AMD architecture, Windows or Linux server.

Some development platforms tried to go one step further and introduced cross-platform virtual environments (e.g. Java), which can run any code built by a Java compiler across any platform. But the main challenge in running complex, multi-service systems for such platforms is that, before you start your services, you have to make sure the infrastructure is installed and configured in the correct way, making it difficult to set up and replicate across multiple installations.

This is where containers come into play. A container is a package that contains your service or application, but in addition also contains the entire environment that your service needs to run. You can think of a container as a small-scale virtual machine (a server) with its own operating system, with all the tools you need pre-installed, and your app code added on top of it. With the advancements in Linux technology, containers are also small in size and have security features that ensure that, even if you run multiple containers on a single (physical or virtual) server, you can be sure that they are running in isolation from one another.

Containers have brought about a fundamental change in how we design, develop and run complex microservices workloads in the cloud:

- Consistency: we can run exactly the same docker container to run applications on a developer workstation as we do in production environments. No more 'it worked on my machine' issues with production code. With the production-like code being run and tested from early stages in development, the number of defects is minimised and a higher quality of tech product is ensured.

- Efficiency: due to the small size and footprint of a typical container, you can now run multiple containers on a single server.

Instead of inefficiently splitting our infrastructure into VMs, each with a specific app or role, you can now use the hardware much more efficiently, but still have the benefit of running a number of containers sharing the core hardware components.

- Scalability: horizontal scaling is the main strength of containers. If your service reaches capacity (say your marketing campaign brings many more customers than anticipated), scaling the service out becomes trivial: all you need to do is spin up another container, and load balance the traffic to it. You can repeat this many times, creating truly highly scalable and available environments. At the same time, you can do this the other way around: if you know that most of your customers use your service in the morning, you can scale up your containers for that period, and then scale down after lunchtime, improving cost-efficiency.

- Flexibility: because containers are environment-agnostic, we can run them on most types of hardware, on premises or on cloud. With the growing popularity of containers, all cloud providers now have offerings that improve and streamline how we manage containers in the cloud. With containers, we can easily use any cloud provider we want, and have the flexibility to move to a different one if required, or run workloads that span cloud providers and on-premises data centres.

Great – so you now have containers, but how do you run them in the cloud? This is the next challenge the development and operations community has been trying to solve, by using container orchestration platforms. As the name suggests, container orchestration platforms are responsible for deploying and managing container workloads in the cloud. There are a number of more or less successful container orchestrators in the world today: Docker Swarm (from the Docker folk), Nomad (from HashiCorp, a well-known name in the automation space), Rancher, and a few others. However, one container platform has seen huge growth in the last few years and has become the leading open source container orchestration platform in the world: Kubernetes.

Originally developed in Google's labs, Kubernetes is now managed by Cloud Native Computing Foundation (CNCF), and is supported natively by all major cloud providers. This ubiquity allows you to deploy Kubernetes' cluster and start managing and scaling services in minutes. In addition to user-friendly web portals, Kubernetes is very much focused on automation, including support for tools such as Terraform for scalable infrastructure-as-a-code management. Being open source and managed by a cloud community, Kubernetes is also free to use, contributing to very wide adoption, a large online community and a wealth of available documentation.

That said, running distributed systems in the cloud is not a trivial task, even with all the tools and support out there. It is important to have a tech team who are comfortable with the technology in question. Due to the specialist knowledge required, in some cases it makes sense to look for external help when setting up future-proof infrastructure for your startup – or at least to start small and lean before expanding as your company grows.

MOBILE WITH FIREBASE

We discussed earlier the need for mobile channel presence for a lot of tech products, and the challenges that mobile strategy brings, the key ones being platform and technology fragmentation, code maintenance overheads and talent availability. Firebase (a startup that was subsequently acquired by Google) is looking to bring a change to that. Firebase is a collection of cloud-based services targeted at mobile developers who want to build cross-platform apps with minimal disruption. The Firebase ecosystem is wide, and some of the most used components within it are:

- Firestore: a cloud-native document database that can be used to build powerful mobile backends without deploying any server code. It also has a real-time database flavour, which streamlines the offline capability of mobile development for when mobile users are in the zone with patchy coverage.

- Authentication: multiple login/signup methods that mobile developers can easily embed into their apps, including username/password, Facebook/Google login, SMS login, etc.

- App distribution: a service for streamlined alpha/beta distribution of your app in a platform-agnostic way, so you can test the app on all major platforms before you start getting into the fragmentation challenges of the iOS App Store and Android Play Store.

A lot of developers use Firebase or similar services, so it's likely that you, as a founder, will come across it sooner or later. Understanding what it offers will give you a head start and make sure you are aligned with the suggestions of your tech team.

DATA: MANAGED DATABASES

Before the cloud, managing databases was a big part of any IT company or department: managing the hardware the databases run on, teams of database administrators owning the data structures, and spending days setting up and tuning the databases to ever-changing data access patterns and workloads.

With the advent of the cloud, this has changed – and for the better. Database is just another service you can buy on demand, renting the capacity that you need and scaling up and down as required.

All cloud providers support some form of managed databases. The question now is, which one do you need and how do you select the right one?

There are a number of established database products available, both commercial and open source, that are well known and understood and have been proven for a long time. Some providers offer these, or at least some flavours of them. For example, you can get MySQL offerings on Azure, AWS or Digital Ocean, and an MS SQL Server on Azure or AWS. Because these database engines are well known, you can use the existing knowledge and experience out there to ensure you use them in the best possible way. The downside is that most of these are not cloud-native, but were developed before cloud became mainstream, so they may lack some cloud-native specific features – mass scale and availability for example. That said, this may only become apparent once you're starting to get closer to millions of users accessing it.

On the other hand, some cloud providers have developed their own cloud-native databases from the ground up based on cloud scalability considerations. The best example of this is GCP, with their CloudSQL and BigQuery. You can be sure these databases can handle anything thrown at them, even if you grow to the size of Google. However, what you do sacrifice is availability of talent – as there are bound to be fewer skilled people familiar with these services – and portability, with support limited to a single cloud provider typically.

A third trend has been emerging recently: developers of most popular databases are building their own cloud offerings specialised to their own database engine. One example is MongoDB Atlas, a cloud service that uses the hardware infrastructure of major cloud providers (you can choose which one), but offering a proven database engine as a service on top of that, run by the people who developed it. In some cases, database engines have been re-engineered to become more cloud-native and offer a good balance of familiarity and proven technology with the mass scale, all at a reasonable cost.

Data storage and management is an important part of startups' tech strategy, and in our view, preserving flexibility is important early on, ensuring access to the right talent or resources for learning. With that in mind, the third, hybrid option seems like a good balance to start with, although your tech team will be able to articulate the best options for their particular use case.

AI AND MACHINE LEARNING

Artificial intelligence (AI) and machine learning (ML) have become some of the most used buzzwords in the IT and startup scene over the last few years. Being able to make sense of data, small and large, make predictions and forecasts, and support supervised and unsupervised learning by machines and software – all of this and more encompasses what AI and ML are.

AI is the broader term, covering anything and everything related to the creation of intelligent systems. ML, on the other hand, covers systems that are able to learn from existing data and behaviour, so ML is a subset of AI.

When you're looking at AI and ML in a cloud context, there are a few considerations that make the relationship with the cloud important:

- Data accessibility, structure and scale: AI and ML work best the more data there is to work with. With cloud computing and managed databases, as discussed earlier, we are now able to collect, interpret and store vast amounts of data in various formats.

- Computing resources: to process such a vast amount of data, we need a lot of computing power – CPU and memory. In the past, getting such power was an expensive capital cost; with the cloud, we can spin the compute resources on demand, scale horizontally, and shut them down once processing is completed in order to save on cost, which is a game changer.

- Everything-as-a-service: we started from infrastructure-as-a-service, then platform-as-a-service, then database-as-a-service (managed databases). It was only a matter of time before we'd be able to have ML-as-a-service or AI-as-a-service, and now a lot of these services do exist. So instead of building your own data lake and processing capability, you can get data scientists to use out-of-the-box cloud services, offering a wide array of data processing, ML and AI features.

This last bullet should be your starting point when thinking about ML and AI in the cloud – what is out there, already available for me to use? – so that you can focus on collecting the valuable data, and use cloud services to process those and gain insights. You can certainly look to build an AI/ML platform by yourself using infrastructure and data building blocks, but before starting on that usually complex journey, check out what out-of-the-box services your cloud provider could offer.

Google Cloud Platform has one of the most comprehensive offerings in this space: the Google AI Platform. Using the standardised data science workflow, it has identified and developed Google cloud services that can help each step of the way: from data ingestion, cleansing and storage, via model development and training, to deployment and validation. The solution relies on many GCP-specific services, making it less portable, but on the other hand Google provides a rich library of resources, documentation and videos, helping your data scientists or tech team get up to speed quickly.

IBM Cloud's famous service IBM Watson is a suite of tools and services that enables AI and ML engineering within the IBM cloud infrastructure. IBM Watson was originally developed as a question answering system within IBM Labs, gaining wider recognition by winning a *Jeopardy!* quiz against human opponents in 2011. It has developed as an AI tech product since, offering a variety of tools such as ML modelling, predictive analytics and forecasting, speech recognition and natural language processing, all as consumable, commoditised service platforms.

AWS has a rich ecosystem of AI-related offerings, albeit a bit more fragmented across separate services with a specific purpose:

- Amazon SageMaker: an integrated IDE and set of services for data scientists to develop, train and deploy ML models.

- Amazon Lex: service for developing bots powered by the same tech as the Alexa voice assistant.

- Amazon Rekognition: for image and video classification and analysis.

Microsoft Azure started slightly later, but is quickly gaining ground with its own Azure AI Platform, including ML tools, cognitive analytics services and a bot development environment.

As you can see, like in other cloud services, AI and ML have seen significant convergence from all main providers towards streamlined offerings of tools and services for data scientists and ML engineers. This sector has not yet seen any standardisation effort (like Kubernetes in the container orchestration space, for example), so portability is still an issue. However, the democratisation of access to such cloud-based AI and ML tools will allow for much faster innovation in this space.

TAKEAWAYS

- The rise of cloud computing has helped address some of the main drawbacks of the process of building and launching a tech product, making it more lean and cost-efficient.

- Convergence and standardisation have helped streamline the offerings and the costs, forcing cloud giants to compete on usability and add-on services instead – it's less important which cloud provider you choose.

- Cloud is not just infrastructure and compute-resource on demand – making use of managed services within the cloud allows startups to use advanced services at reasonable per-use cost, without the need of hiring for specialised skills early on.

- Don't reinvent the wheel – ensure you identify all cloud services you will benefit from, and start using them, instead of building internal capability for these commoditised resources.

PART 2

DELIVERING ON THE PROMISE

7

TECH CHOICES

ERIC CARTER

INTRODUCTION

Tech products are made by using a number of programming languages as a glue for sticking together various combinations of your own bespoke logic, with libraries, frameworks, products and services provided by other parties. There are hundreds of programming languages, each with vast ecosystems of proprietary and open source content of varying levels of quality. NPM, which is the go-to home of reusable code for most Javascript developers, has over one million packages. On top of all that, we have almost limitless choice in how we design and organise our application.

In this chapter, I want to skim the surface of this bewildering ocean of options by talking about some of the factors that can help you decide which options to use, and what can happen if you choose one approach or another.

LANGUAGE SELECTION

Let's start with language selection. Programming languages are designed to be general purpose and Turing complete, meaning that you can build anything in any of them. The choice of language is therefore down to you. Geeks often cite and debate performance as the deciding factor, but with the exception of certain rare and specific scenarios, other softer factors (in my opinion) are far more influential.

At a high level, all languages can be thought of as either typed or dynamic, as well as either compiled or interpreted. As with most classifications, there are shades of grey rather than pure black and white, but for the most part these four quadrants make sense.

TYPED, DYNAMIC, COMPILED AND INTERPRETED LANGUAGES

Typed languages provide a level of security and reassurance that the code you write will work as you expect by preventing a lot of silent errors. For example, a developer may need to compare two times and return the difference as a duration: end time minus start time equals duration. The logic is simple and easily coded by a junior developer; they test it and the result is correct, so they deploy the code and move on to other tasks.

Let us say the developer wrote the code expecting a time in separate hours, minutes and seconds fields. In an untyped language anything goes – there is nothing to stop the input from being the text 'twenty to four'. The developer could write code to check it, but if they feel they trust the input they may not bother.

In a structurally typed language, the input must have the hours, minutes and seconds fields but there is nothing to stop you comparing a local time with a UTC time, so the result may be incorrect depending on the timezone or daylight saving adjustments. In a nominally typed language, local and UTC times are considered different even though they look the same: the language will catch the error.

Typed languages come in roughly two flavours: 1) interpreted languages, which analyse the code when you run the program; and 2) compiled languages, which analyse the code when you build the program.

For our time calculation example, there are three possible ways for the error to occur. A compiled nominally typed language will prevent the developer from building the erroneous program. The interpreted nominally typed language will explicitly raise the error when you run the program, which should be when you test it before releasing. The structurally typed and dynamic languages will both compile and run as if everything is ok, but with an incorrect value in some scenarios.

To catch the error you first need to be aware of the complexities, and then you need to add extra code to identify and handle the complexities and write tests for all the scenarios to build confidence that the implementation is correct. The burden of proof has been shifted from the language to the developer; this immediately opens the door to cutting corners in times of increased pressure, or simply forgetting to add tests when you return from a lunch break.

Given the brief description above, the choice of compiled nominally typed language over dynamic or interpreted languages seems obvious. But some of the most popular languages of recent years, including Javascript and Python, are dynamic interpreted languages. Arguably these languages are simpler to learn and use, and faster for bashing out relatively simple applications.

Javascript has historically been the only option for dynamic web content; the explosion of cloud computing and web products probably does more to explain its current high status. In recent years we have seen options that compile to WebAssembly or transpile to Javascript; with the exception of Typescript these are mostly still immature, requiring a higher level of skill and effort to use effectively.

CLASSIFICATION BASED ON EASE OF USE

Another way to classify languages is on the dimension from easy to hard. This is obviously more subjective, but there is broad agreement in the industry. C++ is designed for run time performance and backwards compatibility with older versions going back decades. For runtime performance, it includes lots of low-level features and behaviours that require the developer to understand how C++ works under the hood. For backwards compatibility the designers have had to keep all the old syntax and behaviour while they added newer, better features; developers therefore need to understand both the old and new ways and why one is better than the other in each situation.

Scala is a far more modern language designed around the functional programming paradigm, but also designed to interoperate and accommodate as much as possible from the more well-known imperative paradigm and Java ecosystem. Scala developers therefore need to understand two fundamentally different ways of computing as well as the large all-encompassing language scope. Scala and C++ have very high learning curves requiring a deep understanding of a lot of things; the benefit of this expertise is the ability to build robust and efficient complex applications.

At the other end of the spectrum is Golang, a modern language designed specifically to be easy to use. They have kept the language itself so small that it has been said it is the only language you can fit in your head. For example, where other languages provide multiple ways of looping over data, Golang provides only one. Don't think that because the language is simple it can only be used for simple applications; it is still very capable and complete and extensively used in complex industries. Sometimes less is more. As well as being easy to learn, the reduced number of options means there is much more consistency across developer styles.

This reminds me of a schism in one of my old dev teams: one of the developers had an abstract style, and another developer a concise style. They would reject each other's code in reviews and have arguments in meetings. The clash poisoned the team, reduced productivity and made others feel uncomfortable. If we had been using Golang, I doubt there would have been such a difference in approach.

LANGUAGE SELECTION FOR STARTUPS

Nothing we have discussed about language selection so far has been specific to startups. I came from a typical large established company that was organised into multiple teams specialised in different languages targeted at the different components: Android developers, web developers and backend Java developers, etc. The macro management was driven mostly by utilisation: when a project came up, if there was a Java team available, Java would be used for the backend.

Similarly, as a Java developer you would be pigeonholed and pushed into Java projects. Within each project team, if the workload was not perfectly balanced across all the tech specialisms, someone would become a linchpin, responsible for the dependencies of the bulk of a piece of work, while others in the team wouldn't or couldn't switch roles to help out.

There were usually enough rounded, driven, eager-to-learn individuals who would glue the teams together by taking on whatever role was needed, but these people often had grander ambitions and eventually found themselves stifled by the company's reluctance to adopt new technologies, because of their desire to fully utilise the existing talent pool.

Many of the startups we help at thestartupfactory.tech initially have no team, no product and no money to pay the salaries of expert developers. You may identify with this, and if you do you'll know that your priorities are significantly different from the established company with an existing team to protect and utilise. Instead, you need to maximise your ability to recruit a small team, utilise it well, and deliver quickly to start bringing in revenue. Startups also need to plan for rapid expansion and change within both the product and the team. We help to pick the tech and build the team from scratch; recruiting the team is the hard part.

By selecting modern, popular and accessible languages that are of interest to eager, motivated developers, we make the job of recruitment much easier (although we usually want to avoid straying into emerging, unproven, hipster tech territory). Furthermore we can maximise the flexibility of small teams and minimise the learning overhead by selecting a single language that works well for all the components of the application.

LIBRARIES AND COMPONENTS

We have spoken briefly and quite dryly about the different dimensions of programming languages, but ultimately language selection happens near the start of a project and rarely changes from then on. As product development continues and new features are added, there are countless opportunities to select existing libraries or components from a choice of thousands, or to build your own.

Last year we had an intern working with us at thestartupfactory.tech; he was a great, motivated, capable, computer science undergraduate from Manchester University. In many ways, I would say he was the archetype of the sort of junior developer that I've seen in many teams and would like to see again and again in future. He was fast, maybe too fast, and even his speech clocked in at about 300 words per minute (apparently the average is 125–150 words per minute, and JFK had a world record for hitting 327 words in one minute of a speech).

When our super intern took on a task, he would Google it, read the TLDR and soon after be using some library or component pulled from a public repository, while I was still making my morning brew. Productivity was up, at least in the short term. As the CEO of a small startup, you don't want to stifle this productivity with committees, processes and micromanagement; however, you and your development team should be conscious of some of the signposts and consequences of selecting one third-party library over another, so let's look at some.

One of our recent clients came with an application built using Apache Cordova and a number of Cordova plugins. Cordova is a solution that packages a web page into Android and iOS apps to save you from having to develop independent versions using the Android and iOS native languages, which is a massive benefit to a startup racing to release an app.

Cordova was by no means niche, and being part of the Apache Software Foundation meant it should be reliably maintained. In the fast-moving world of tech, Cordova's popularity has waned, and although Cordova has been updated in line with iOS and Android, its plugin authors have not kept up: none of the plugins on the first page of the site have been updated in the last thousand days.

By relying on a plugin that was not actively maintained, our clients tied themselves to an old version of Cordova, which in turn prevented them from keeping their app up to date with Android and iOS. When you decide to use a third-party library there is a trade-off: you avoid a potentially significant development and maintenance cost, but with a loss of control over part of your realm.

You need to be prepared to respond to the changing tech landscape, which in some rare cases can be a significant chunk of work. The risk of such events is inversely proportional to the size of the library's backers and the number of users of an open source component. The number of users is also a good proxy for how well tested and reliable the library is, and how much educational content will have been published for it.

I studied electronic engineering at Cardiff University: the first programming course was in C, and there were practicals but it was mostly delivered in a lecture hall on a chalkboard. In the exam, we had to write syntactically correct code with pen on paper while sat isolated at our small square tables.

I can hardly think of a less realistic scenario in which to be assessed. Out in the real world, developers use editors that lift the syntax burden by automatically colouring, indenting and even auto-inserting the squiggly and square brackets that liberally weave through the code. The vast majority of professional developers have multiple screens, one showing their code and one with their preferred search engine. We developers constantly search the documentation of the tools we are using, check the finer details of how to articulate what we are thinking in that language, seek out new libraries and new frameworks, and visit blogs and tutorials from other people who have already solved our problems.

When the documentation is lacking, and the blogs and examples are hard to find, you are left in the dark. Problems take much longer to solve, and you miss out on the discussions, the alternatives proposed by others, and the insights of those who have tried and failed. The quality of the official documentation and the size of the community who use and write about a particular technology are of the utmost importance when you select a language, platform or framework for your team. Fortunately many providers understand this importance and put substantial effort into providing a good set of resources, so there are lots to choose from.

When choosing an open source or third-party component, especially if it is playing a key role in your system, ask yourself who maintains it — one person, a small unknown company, or a big industry heavyweight? How often is it updated? How many users does it have? Is there good documentation and a lot of user-generated content? Answering such questions will help you make a better choice between two or more potential options.

SHOULD YOU CREATE YOUR OWN SOLUTION?

When the choice is between using an existing implementation and rolling out your own solution, it's almost always best to reuse the existing solution. I have gone both ways on this multiple times; my inner demon comes out when I need something reasonably simple. Either I just see a solution and dive into coding it, or I look into available solutions but lazily back out of learning a large API when I only need a small part.

But then after the initial burst of creativity, when I find myself churning out boilerplate code, writing tests, debugging issues and quite frequently uncovering a whole layer of unanticipated complexity, I regret the lazy initial decision. Even small open source projects have usually had hundreds of hours invested into them, have been tried and tested in numerous real-world scenarios, and – significantly – will continue to be improved and maintained for free.

Conversely there have been occasions, one very recently, where having initially used an open source component and run with it successfully for months, I then tried to make a seemingly simple change and things broke. After hours of investigation and diving into the open source code, I found that the implementation was very basic, making assumptions about a certain way of working that were no longer valid for my scenario.

It initially looked like a significant effort to actually improve the component myself, but afterwards, with a better understanding of the magic behind the façade, it was reasonably quick to replace the external component with a bespoke alternative. By selecting an open source component at the start, I quickly got the system working and released, without locking myself into a particular implementation. That way, when the need arose further down the line, I could take on the additional effort of creating a bespoke solution.

APPLICATIONS SOFTWARE ARCHITECTURE

The last thing I want to talk about in this chapter is your application's software architecture (for more detail on this see Chapter 5). There are plenty of general software architecture texts available, so I'll jump straight into startup specifics and one appropriate architecture: microservices.

More than other companies, startups are embarking on a journey into the unknown with limited resources. Your ability to work quickly, respond to lessons by changing direction and priority, to grow and expand your product and company, and your ability to make the best balance of tactical and strategic moves are all going to massively influence your startup's level of success.

Without planning, it is all too easy to organically grow your product by bolting on more and more features and more and more code. The likely result of this unguided approach is one large monolithic application filled with complexity that constrains your future deployment options and your future recruitment options. I know because I've done it, and it is especially common in junior teams lacking in architectural pedigree.

When a task needs to be done, it is much quicker to add a function here that pulls data from there, rather than to create a whole new service that separates out the different areas of functionality and integrates through a newly designed API. But if you can, with a little bit of thought, divide your application up into lots of smaller simpler parallel applications; you can improve your flexibility so much that the knock-on impacts are revolutionary. Let me explain with a case study drawn from a very promising startup currently under thestart-upfactory.tech's wing.

The product takes data from remote sensors and makes it available to the owners wherever they are. The naive approach would be to have two components, one for the sensor and one for the cloud service, with most of the functionality implemented in the cloud service. In contrast, the microservices approach we used has the sensor service, a data processor service, a data aggregator, a data presentation service, a user management service, a sensor management service and a monitoring alarm service.

This allowed us to use a different language for the processor component so we could select a specialised open source library while keeping most of the application in a more accessible and appropriate language. We can now make changes to small parts of the application without a full re-release, and we can deploy multiple instances of any component if that component has significantly more workload. Similarly, if one component develops an issue, only part of the application may suffer; for example, you may not be able to view data, but the data is still being recorded and will be available when the issue is resolved.

The enforced structure in the application makes it easier for us to make better decisions and harder to hack in dodgy short-sighted fixes. The structure also makes the system easier to understand and reason about, giving us an immediate benefit in productivity. Looking to the future, we have the option of porting or refactoring one component at a time rather than having to take on the whole system. As the team grows we can give ownership of specific components to individuals, helping their personal development as well as delegating responsibility from a central single point of failure.

TAKEAWAYS

- Consider your current and future team when making tech selections, such as what language to use.

- Use open source components, choose them wisely and be prepared for change. Or, if it's the right decision, build your own.

- Look to the future by planning and building your application with flexibility so that you can adapt to whatever changes come your way, either in your business or in the tech world as a whole.

8
ENGINEERING PROCESS
ERIC CARTER

INTRODUCTION

The engineering process often includes what seem to be counterintuitive activities, such as refactoring (which involves repeating yourself) and regular releases (perhaps before the product seems ready). However, in this chapter, we'll show how such processes can improve quality and productivity, even though it might feel like they'd do the opposite. For those readers new to software development processes, let's start by showing you how to recognise what the default software development process is with a summary of its key features. You can usually think of these progressing through four stages: plan, build, release and maintenance.

- The plan stage includes defining requirements or 'user stories'; estimating time to complete; some level of design, from formal reviewed documentation to a basic napkin sketch.

- The build stage chunks up large work and divides it between developers to write the code, and often includes some level of local testing.

- Then comes the release stage, which includes activities such as: grouping together chunks of developed code; testing activities; code reviews; security audits; and the actual application deployment.

- The last stage is maintenance and support, which is usually a vaguely defined ongoing activity frequently palmed off onto another group

I have seen variations on this approach in all companies and most projects or proposals. This includes 'agile' projects, where this process is merely repeated in a loop incrementally, building new features or adding updates. The details are not that important: the significant features are its linearity and optimism. Linearity because there is a sequence of steps all moving in one direction. Optimism because testing activities are treated as gate conditions that are expected to be passed, rather than learning opportunities expected to influence the future direction of the project.

'PROJECT MERCURY'

Ten or so years ago in 2010, when I was a junior engineer, I worked on a project codenamed 'Mercury'. I use the term codenamed in its literal sense as the project details were restricted by national security classifications, so forgive me for skipping over the specifics.

The Mercury project has stuck in my memory as one of the most enjoyable and successful I've worked on. There was an interesting core puzzle to solve – I remember drawing numerous square boxes on squared paper to visualise the solution through slowly squaring eyes. There was real detailed research into the depths of protocol specifications and custom hardware to understand and account for all the edge conditions. And there were significant performance challenges to keep up with the rate of data. But the most important thing was how we approached the project.

From the outset, the project was scheduled in three phases. Phase 1 was a short proof-of-concept implementation that only needed to show that the main aim and approach was feasible. Phase

2 was to build the solution, solving all the problems, covering all the edge cases, and providing all the interfaces. Phase 3 is where it got interesting. The goal of Phase 3 was simply to start again and rebuild Phase 2 with no new features and no increase in performance. It sounds like a total waste of time, but there was method in the madness.

When we were implementing Phase 2, we didn't know exactly what we were doing, only what we wanted to achieve and how we anticipated it working. As with all projects there were unknowns, things we did not realise or anticipate, detailed interactions that didn't quite work out. When this happens you need to pause to think, and then you either bolt on an extra bit of code, make an extra API call, add some special magical message type, or go back and change some other code a little or a lot. The result is a codebase that is more convoluted and brittle than you would like, that runs a bit too slow and exposes a bit too much information.

REFACTORING

Fortunately we had Phase 3: this time we had no unknowns, we knew the pinch points, and with the benefit of hindsight we knew how we could have done better. Reworking the implementation in Phase 3 is an activity known as refactoring; this may result in higher quality and performance but the main aim is usually to simplify, organise and tidy the code to make it easier to understand, fix, change and extend as the product grows in the future. Think of it as investment now, repaid in higher productivity in the future. And, similar to financial investments, the returns have compound interest.

Refactoring is usually an afterthought, constantly requested by developers and deprioritised in favour of new features until a critical level is reached, at which point the refactoring activity has to be scheduled, pushing new feature work back.

In the Mercury project we planned it in from the start. The proactive approach is more honest for project accounting, as we recognise the technical debt incurred rather than silently deferring it to future features. But the real benefit of scheduling a pre-planned refactor is that it actually made Phase 2 (the initial development) quicker to complete. The reason for this probably has a name and many studies in psychology circles, but I don't know them. I call it the finishing hurdle or completion fear, and with no evidence to back me up I will confidently invoke the 80/20 rule, that the last 20% of a project takes 80% of the time.

We humans find it hard to stop and say 'that will do'. We stress about text positions, trying many options to find the perfect fit. We want to polish the output to be something that we are proud of. We feel the need to solve all the niggles that we anticipate might be a problem, even though we don't yet know whether they will actually cause an issue.

During Phase 2 of the Mercury project, we knew we had Phase 3 to finalise things, so we were not constantly up against a finishing line for every section of code, which liberated us from our inner perfectionist demons. Instead of fussing over a precise layout, we could do something pretty good and move on. When we had ideas about improvements, we could shelve them. And when we got stuck on some weird and wonderful bug, we could choose to hack around it and defer the real fix until we knew more about whether it would be a problem or even if that code would make the final cut.

HOW IMPORTANT IS REFACTORING?

I am sure that some of you are thinking that this all sounds reasonable; but how marginal are the returns and is it really worth postponing a revenue-creating feature?

Just over a year ago I picked up a project that had already completed an initial build; they had a few more features to add and a few creases to iron out. This project contained an image processing component to extract a measurable feature from an image. The algorithm implemented to achieve this was a little over two hundred lines of code that took the image through numerous stages to arrive at its result.

It was pretty clever and worked well in a few scenarios, but it failed spectacularly in others and it was almost impossible to understand why it reached those strange results. Initially I planned on tweaking it a bit and adding some feedback to help us to understand the strange operation. Instead, I thought up a totally different algorithm and implemented it in just six lines of code.

The result was a little more accurate and reliable than the original version but still gave crazy results in some situations, but this time it was easy to understand why. You could look at an image and replay the algorithm roughly in your head to understand and explain what feature was throwing the result off. In this instance the refactored code was two orders of magnitude smaller than the original.

So what happens if you don't refactor? There are lots of examples out there of organisations large and small that have suffered due to their short-sighted prioritisations. The last project at my previous job was a very expensive full system replacement for an old Cobol mainframe system that should have been phased out decades ago. That company was left behind technically because they couldn't easily add new features, and they were massively at risk of issues with their current system because everyone in the world who knew Cobol had retired.

But things don't always take that long to become an issue: this year we were asked to help a startup who, for just a couple of years, had focused far too much on customer features. Technology changes very rapidly and takes developers along with it: this startup company probably started with some slightly old tech and then failed to keep up with the changes, leaving them running versions that were incompatible with the latest devices used by their customers. Their tech debt was mounting rapidly.

Their staff were spending all of their time in a high-stress environment, fighting to meet release deadlines, respond to issues and make maintenance updates to keep up with the latest iOS and Android versions. Things had become so bad that all of the developers ended up handing in their resignations, and the startup faced a very immediate and painful problem of their own making.

These anecdotes show that the impact of refactoring can be significant, and that the impact of ignoring technical debt can be crippling. The Mercury story explained the benefits of a refactor on quality and future productivity, and also explained how pre-scheduling that refactor increases the speed of feature development.

BALANCING THE AMOUNT OF TIME SPENT REFACTORING

Hopefully you have been convinced of the benefits of refactoring, and of proactively anticipating and planning for it, and you're now asking yourself how to go about it.

There is obviously a balance to be struck between how much time should be spent on new features versus refactoring. You should certainly be spending most of your time on new features. The cost of software development is not primarily in the typing time, it is in the time it takes to understand the problem, uncover the unknowns and design solutions, and the time it takes to test, document and communicate.

Refactoring is far more weighted towards design and typing time as you don't need to re-investigate the problem and you will already have implemented a set of tests. You should therefore anticipate refactoring to take only a fraction of the total time of initial development.

So what should you refactor and when? In a sense, I think that these questions miss the point by treating the refactor as a standalone bolt-on to your process rather than being integral to it. Think of the refactor pattern as similar to the MVP philosophy (covered in Chapter 2). The MVP is a core system which is then incrementally extended with additional features over subsequent releases as we learn more about its operation and its users. The refactor starts with a reasonable implementation and iteratively improves the quality as we learn more throughout the build. When integrated into your way of working, you will refactor everything newly added in every release, from small individual functions to large-scale architectural organisations.

RELEASE AND MAINTENANCE

The previous paragraphs on refactoring were mostly focused on the first two stages of the default software development process, plan and build. I would now like to talk a little about the final two stages, release and maintenance. Before you read on, make a cup of tea and take a few moments to think about the activities you anticipate your startup completing over the next few years.

Welcome back. I am guessing that most of you thought about a roadmap of features for future releases, growing your customer base and also growing your team. But how many of you were thinking about bug fixes and security patches, making updates to allow your product to continue working with new OS releases and other third-party API updates, or even making a change to appease key customers or conform to new legislation? There are a lot of these sorts of unexpected maintenance activities that will happen again and again; fortunately they are usually quite small and simple changes, but you will need to be ready to respond quickly.

The situation of the startup with technical debt, mentioned in the refactoring section above, was amplified by – or even caused by – their development process. They thought only about their product and the features their clients requested, and not about updates, fixes or patches – i.e. maintenance. This meant there was never enough time to upgrade the product across the board – not with new features, but to comply with the new tech and operating systems.

In addition, their process for new product releases was all manual. They had their features built and knew that they needed to test their product. But they thought of testing as simply a hurdle to be passed, and hence they chose the quick bolt-on approach of manual testing in order to release as quickly as possible. Manual tests are easy to start but they are not free in terms of time: it takes time to click through all the steps and record the outputs, and the final outcome of that invested time is simply a pass/fail status.

Similarly they took the same manual, lowest barrier to entry approach to deploying their new product release. When problems inevitably surfaced, and when new feature requests and maintenance updates appeared on the to-do list, they had nothing to fall back on and had to repeat the same time-consuming manual processes.

AUTOMATION

Automation is by far the most significant investment you can make in your processes. It certainly takes more initial effort to get going and comes with its own maintenance cost, but the benefits vastly outweigh the costs. Automated processes are faster to execute, they remove the human error factor replacing it with precisely repeatable steps, and they free your team from time-consuming mundane activities. Those are just some of the first-order benefits, and it's what these benefits in turn enable that makes automation a game changer.

The Cobol system replacement project I worked on a few years ago was a pretty major undertaking. I led a team of 50 developers over three years just to build the first release. The stakes were high for the client and they naturally wanted everything to be right before they switched to the new system. In such a large project, issues are all but guaranteed: we had made some mistakes, and they had forgotten to tell us some things etc., so they decided to delay the release until these problems were resolved.

Then there was a commercially sensitive period, so they decided to delay the release till this had passed; since there was a development team sitting there, we decided we might as well continue with updates and improvements, and so more errors crept in and the release was delayed further. Then the client's circumstances changed and they had to add some new requirements, delaying the release again to accommodate them.

We started to feel like the client was stalling: they were too fearful of releasing, and every time they delayed and increased the scope, the risk and the fear grew larger. Eventually, and with some pressure from senior figures on both sides, the project team accepted that no system can be perfect and that the risks were manageable. In the end, the release went surprisingly smoothly.

At thestartupfactory.tech we embrace automation and build our engineering and delivery process around what the industry calls 'continuous integration' (CI). This allows a developer to take on a small piece of work, then the CI system automatically runs a large suite of tests to check that previously working features are still working; and if they are, the CI system automatically deploys the new code to the fleets of servers and devices of the real user systems.

This setup allows us to make multiple releases every day. Because each release is small, there is a lower risk of it containing issues, the impact of issues is usually much reduced to only the area of the change, and any issues that do occur are easier to find and fix in the smaller change set. The old adage says that 'practice makes perfect': people who regularly release code and regularly fix issues will be better at it than people who do it only rarely with infrequent massive releases.

Automation is a game-changer because it allows you to change how you run your business. It enables you to build an interactive relationship with your customers by responding to their issues within hours. And having a large automated test suite gives your developers the confidence to make changes quickly, and to refactor freely, as described earlier in this chapter, without stressing about unintended consequences, because you know the tests will catch them. There are even companies that have decided they can cut out the overhead of testing entirely by having a slick process for releasing to sets of real users, monitoring the impact and quickly resolving any issues.

WHERE TO GO FROM HERE

Successful tech companies treat their process as their product. They are proactive tech companies rather than reactive product companies. They differentiate themselves from competitors with similar products by staying ahead of the curve, keeping ahead of changing landscapes and responding to their customers' changing needs. Their value is built into their company, not in one product, allowing them to diversify and expand.

As the CEO of a tech startup, you may have limited experience of building software products, engineering processes or managing development teams. You may have a small team with capable developers but no one experienced at the CTO level. But as a founder, you should now be able to think about setting the strategic goals and priorities for your company, and have some idea of whether a high level of automation, a fast release frequency and iterative refactoring are the right way to run your process.

TAKEAWAYS

- Building a tech product is not a one-time activity: the tech landscape and your product are constantly shifting, and your process needs to reflect that.

- Some successful strategies are counterintuitive; to find them you need to be bold and experiment.

- Refactoring and maintenance may seem to slow down the addition of new features, but will in fact save time in the long run.

- Automation is a game-changer well worth investing in early and building upon throughout.

9

BUILDING THE TECH TEAM

ALEKSA VUKOTIC

INTRODUCTION

It's been said that great people make great companies, and nothing is truer than that in the startup world. Even with the best ideas and a strong vision, to make them a reality, build a world-class tech product, disrupt the industry and innovate for the greater good, we need to surround ourselves with great people. That means a great team specialising in software engineering, one of the most in-demand skills in the world. In this chapter, we'll share some of our experience and know-how in attracting and developing good tech talent.

CHALLENGES IN BUILDING THE STARTUP TECH TEAM

Assembling an excellent tech team is a challenge for most companies, and startups in particular have their own set of challenges. For early-stage startups the biggest challenge is usually the budget: operating on a shoestring budget does not allow you to bring in world-class professionals who will likely receive a high salary elsewhere.

Another challenge is the strategy: startups need to be lean and build quick proofs of concept and MVPs (minimum viable products) to demonstrate and validate ideas, often by taking many shortcuts early on. However, they also need to be focused on long-term strategy and technical viability: building a quality tech product requires time, and thinking about technology vision and strategy requires a longer-term view. Skills and personal values that satisfy both the short-term, all-hands-on-deck, multi-disciplinary approach and the more thoughtful, strategic vision, including more complex technology stack and process, are hard to find in a single person or team.

Finally, startups typically work hard and quickly to deliver the first version of a product – an MVP. After the MVP has been launched, there is a period of reflection, measurement, testing and validation, ensuring product market-fit, collecting user feedback, validating the decisions made and ascertaining any needed changes in strategy in the future.

It's possible that the results of this reflection phase are brilliant, and we just continue on. However, it's more likely that changes will be needed, whether in the product itself or the business model and offering that will require redesigning and rebuilding at least parts of the tech product, which in turn will require more time to think and plan ahead. In many situations it's wasteful to have a tech team in this phase. Ideally we could pause development, minimising the cost to the business until we're clear how to proceed.

So, ideally, a startup would want a motivated, knowledgeable team that can build things quickly in the short term, can be paused post-MVP launch, and then take on a more strategic engineering approach when required. A tough ask!

Let's see how we can approach the challenge of tech team building, first by looking at the role of the technology stack and vision in attracting the right talent early on.

ROLE OF TECHNOLOGY CHOICES

Technology vision and strategy have a critical impact on the hiring strategy and team building activities in two key ways, which we'll discuss in this section: using technology as a motivational and talent acquisition tool; and making sure that technology choices are streamlined to improve the efficiency of team expansion.

As mentioned before, in order to build a world-class team in any professional sphere, you need to make sure that individual members' goals and common goals are aligned. If you're building a football team to challenge for trophies, you need players with the right attitude, but also players who are motivated by, and enjoy, the way the team plays on the field.

Similarly, to build a world-class tech product in a startup environment, you need a technology team that is not only motivated and aligned with the startup's vision and goals, but who will enjoy the challenges and problem-solving that comes from using technology as a key part of the daily job. It has become a trend in software engineering and development that the brightest talent does not want a job that is well paid and nothing more, but one that employs cutting-edge technology, and offers opportunities to learn and to constantly improve while doing what they enjoy the most — typing code in front of a screen and solving engineering and usability challenges.

Based on what we just said, it's unlikely that you'll attract the best talent if you're consigned to building your tech product using legacy technology, or by involving a lot of manual or repetitive work. So making the right technology choices not only influences the quality of the tech product, but ensures that talented people enjoy using that stack to build the founder's vision.

Sometimes, that means using unproven or bleeding-edge technology against a common wisdom of going for proven and well-established tools — and that's fine! Taking risks with some technology choices for the benefit of building a motivated team can be a good bet for the future of company growth and the team. At the same time, cutting-edge, unproven technology with a lot of potential is a great innovation driver, ensuring you stay on top of the game as the product and technology landscape evolves.

That said, this needs a balanced approach: using only unproven technology will help in having a motivated and engaged tech team, but can also detract from the lean focus on product delivery. So, in order to succeed, you need to balance these two needs, and have a trusted tech leadership within the company that will help you with this task.

The second key role of technology when it comes to hiring and team composition is maintaining a focus that allows for a smaller team to begin with that can scale over time as you grow. How do you achieve that?

The key goal is to streamline technology choices, and not proliferate many different tech solutions for different parts of the product, even though product complexity may warrant it.

Let's take an example of a typical tech platform with a backend, web front-end, and a mobile app. There are a variety of technologies to choose from for each of these components. You can build backends in almost any programming language or framework you can think of – Java/Spring, .NET, Go, Javascript/NodeJs, Python, etc. Web front-ends are nowadays mainly built in Javascript frameworks like React or Vue, but you can also use ASP.net or ScalaJS. Mobile apps can be developed using native approaches with Java/Kotlin/ Objective C/Swift or cross-platform frameworks such as React-Native, Xamarin or Flutter. Typically, a startup will go with whatever tech their first tech hires are familiar with, then expand the stack as the team grows. This can produce some quick results, but often ends with a patchwork of technologies that is difficult to maintain and requires a bigger team due to all the different skills required.

A better option would be taking a more strategic approach: have a look at a common technology that can give you the most bang for your buck across all components, and go for it. Then build a team with relevant skills around it. In our example above, we'd typically go with a JavaScript/Reach stack: you can use Javascript to build robust and scalable yet simple backend REST APIs; it's a major tech for anything web-related, and if you use React and React-Native, you'll have some commonality within the Javascript ecosystem across both web and mobile app components. A simpler, more streamlined technology stack will result not only in a simpler and more cost-effective product build, but will give a better strategic structure to your hiring plans.

You can focus on key personnel looking for broad knowledge across Javascript, and you can build an efficient process for onboarding and training more junior team members focused on a single technology at its core.

This doesn't mean that you have to use a single technology across the product. There will inevitably be some components that are geared toward different tech choices (for example, Python if you're looking for data analytics and machine learning), and that's fine; we can specialise in more focused areas while keeping the core within the single tech ecosystem.

We've only touched on software development choices here as an example. In reality, you need to apply similar thinking to other aspects of tech product engineering: deployments and operations, or databases and general data strategy. There is just not enough space in this book to discuss all of this, but the same principles will apply, and you can learn more by looking at other thestartupfactory.tech resources and publications.

TECH PARTNERSHIPS

The especially difficult part of building a team is choosing the first hires, those who will define not only the first iteration of the product but the company and its culture as a whole.

Startups have an additional challenge in that process — a small budget in the early stages — and also a desire to pause and reflect once an MVP has been launched. Imagine building a tech team of five to create an MVP and launch it. Typically, the startup would pause for a bit at that point to test and evaluate the proposition and decide on the next steps in the product journey. Unless you have investors with deep pockets, having a talented but expensive tech team twiddling their thumbs while you evaluate is neither efficient nor cost-effective. Even if you make up new features that will keep the team busy, or address tech debt during this time, it could all be wasted effort if, for example, your MVP evaluation proves that you need to pivot.

In order to address these problems, some startups take the decision to build an MVP using a team of contractors or temporary hires. While this gives some flexibility, it is usually more expensive to begin with, and a mercenary approach to the development won't contribute to company culture or help with future hiring plans.

So, how do we create an excellent product, build a company culture while doing so, and take a break after launching it, all while retaining the relationships and access to talent?

Our suggestion is tech partnerships. Finding culturally like-minded companies whose teams know and understand technology and are able to access or attract engineering talent could be a golden ticket for an early-stage startup that doesn't have the resources to build a world-class team at this stage, but has the vision and ambition to do so in the future.

At thestartupfactory.tech, one of the key roles we play with the founders we work with is that of trusted tech partner and advisor. Someone to be relied on to build the MVP, but also to help hire the right talent when the time comes, mentoring and guiding them to shape that company culture from the beginning, and with the added flexibility of pausing and continuing when required. We also provide ongoing support, which may be of great value to a non-tech founder especially, whose focus is on product or sales and marketing activities to grow the company.

If you do decide to look for a technology partner to help you out on your journey, there is one thing that's important to understand: you are looking for a *partner*, not a supplier. In software development, it is easy to get bogged down in supplier/customer relationships, and it is our strong belief that this does not work in the startup environment. While software delivery companies (suppliers) can do an excellent job in quickly building a tech product, what you, as a startup founder, are looking for is more.

If you are ambitious in seeking to achieve your founder's vision, in addition to creating an MVP, you also need to set the company right so it can grow and develop a team of its own, maybe starting with less experienced but highly motivated team members who will be coached and mentored by your tech partner to develop your culture. And that's a key difference between a supplier and a partner relationship: make sure you approach your tech partner with a clear understanding of your expectations so you can get the most out of it.

BALANCING THE TEAM: PRODUCTIVITY AND CULTURE

The final topic we're going to discuss is how to structure and balance the tech team, and ensure long-term cohesion, motivation and productivity.

Having a world-class, self-managed team requires there to be a certain level of skill and experience within the team. The most productive dev teams I have worked with were relatively small in size (five to six team members at most), but had strong general engineering skills, excellent specialist knowledge and the cultural capacity to adapt to changing circumstances and organise their work themselves. I used to say: 'Give me a team of five that I can handpick and we'll rebuild the internet.' While this is slightly exaggerating, the productivity and quality of the output of such a team makes it seem like anything is possible.

There are a few challenges with building such an experienced and well-organised team. First, it takes time: finding talent is difficult, and enabling the organic growth of such a team requires time and patience – often years. The second challenge, and this is more pertinent to the realities of an early-stage startup, is that it's expensive, either in monetary terms or in equity percentages; whatever is required to attract the right people. It's so prohibitively expensive, in fact, that it's almost impossible to base your tech hiring strategy on that approach.

The alternative is to use a common piece of wisdom in startup circles: to begin with, find beginners, less skilled and experienced engineers who have the hunger and motivation to learn and build tech products at a much lower cost. And this seems like a reasonable strategy: deliver the MVP as quickly and cheaply as possible, and once an idea has been proven on the market, look for investment to improve the quality and long-term maintainability of the software.

However, in our experience, this can be a double-edged sword. First, such 'hacky' approaches to developing a tech product often result in poor quality, affecting the level of impact the MVP can have on the market. In addition, the lower quality and shortcuts taken would mean significant effort would be required to rebuild later, making the initial process less lean, and even affecting the sentiments of investors if their inevitable due diligence process reports a number of red flags.

Finally, even if post-MVP there is a budget to build a higher-quality team to reboot the product, the impact on the existing, less-experienced team could be significant, as they could see themselves as superseded by new outsiders, affecting the long-term team dynamics and culture within the company.

We are advocates of a more balanced approach, appreciative of the budget constraints in a startup world, but aware of the importance of the tech team, culture and build quality of the MVP for the long-term future of any tech-minded company.

One way to address this, as we've mentioned, is using tech partnerships to provide seasoned engineers who can be productive and at the same time mentor the less experienced engineers within your team. Another way is to make your first engineering hire someone who's been around the block and understands the tech landscape and how to navigate it, even if they're not a superstar developer by any means.

The important skills you are looking for are broad technical knowledge, a mentoring personality and willingness to grow the team around them. Then you can look to match this with a more junior hire, looking at their willingness to learn and motivation to join a fast-moving startup – not solely at their school grades and test results. And then continue that process. Any junior hire should be matched with a more experienced engineer to ensure the capacity of the team for productive delivery, but also to ensure a culture of learning and improvement.

Continuous improvement is the key cultural attribute you want your team to excel in. Being passionate about tech and about the product, looking to improve both the product and themselves as the company grows, will ensure high job satisfaction. Investing in books, conference attendance and meetups (as a team), will help with social cohesion and maintain the thirst for knowledge. Eventually, some of the engineers may want to put themselves out there and start blogging or presenting at tech events; this should be encouraged, as it not only improves the attractiveness of the role, but it builds your brand and awareness of the company in the tech community, helping with the hiring process in the future.

One final comment: the tech team is the heart of a tech company (or a company building a tech product); they should be treated as such. Do not expect the development team to be banished to a back room where they can do their 'techie stuff': they should be in the thick of everything, in front of clients and customers and participating in commercial decisions and marketing activities – their input can be invaluable.

TAKEAWAYS

- Building an excellent tech team is a prerequisite to building a great tech company or product.

- Technology choices impact the hiring process: working with the latest tech and innovative tools increases the attractiveness of your engineering proposition (and will improve your product too).

- A great team will consist of both seasoned engineers and less experienced developers – if experienced engineers are out of reach of your budget, work with a tech partner to provide access to tech talent who will speed up your MVP and mentor your less experienced team at the same time.

- A culture of constructive feedback and continuous learning and improvement should be baked in from the start, ensuring a great future for the team.

10

AGILE PROJECT MANAGEMENT

JAMES BROOKES

INTRODUCTION

'Vision without action is a daydream, but action without vision is a nightmare.' (Japanese proverb)

Process is one of the most challenging aspects of a business or idea to get right and is fundamental to successful and efficient operations. With so much pressure and jargon on a subject such as process, it can be very difficult to even know where to start, let alone begin to tailor a process to your specific needs – just look below.

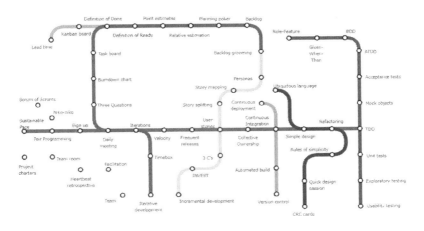

Lines represent practices from the various Agile "tribes" or areas of concern:

In this chapter, we'll go over some of the fundamental concepts common to all 'agile' processes (see, there's the first piece of jargon), and then how these base processes can be expanded to ensure that not only is the best software being built in the most effective way, but also that the main purpose of the software is kept front and centre in your thinking – the customer experience.

DESIGN SPRINT

The first and most difficult task at times should be carried out before any building has even happened – do other people actually see value in what you want to do? That doesn't sound so difficult, I hear you say. The reason it is difficult is that sometimes people won't see value in what you're doing, and the idea you've been nurturing and putting hope into doesn't get off the ground at the first hurdle. Hopefully, the feedback will be constructive and positive but be prepared if it isn't; the road to creating a startup is full of these knocks.

So we know the what, but the how is equally important so as to maximise the utility of the feedback while giving users the best opportunity to understand the value of what you are offering. In order to deliver on the how, a process was developed by Jake Knapp at Google Ventures called the 'Design Sprint'[16]. The base premise is to help understand, design, build and test an idea in just five days through prototyping.

The book *Sprint* gives a full overview of the five-day process and the outcomes anyone going through the process should look to come out with. At thestartupfactory.tech, we have practised this process with many startups to help refine and then further develop their idea through rapid prototyping and iterative feedback and improvement

16 Knapp J., Kowitz B., Zeratsky J., 10 March 2016, *Sprint: How To Solve Big Problems and Test New Ideas in Just Five Days*, Bantam Press

loops. Alongside this, we have added additional features to look at other aspects of the business, such as the value proposition canvas (VPC), business model canvas (BMC) and the technical strategy. This has been dubbed the Startup Sprint©.

Having battled through the arduous process of either a Design Sprint or a Startup Sprint© (they are incredibly taxing mentally), it's time to get out of the building and test and iterate. This will form a theme throughout the chapter: that the build-test-learn iteration is key to not only a good technical product that fulfils the needs of customers, but also to creating a process that is tailor-made to your team.

TRUE AGILE

When it comes to tailor-making a process for your team, there are a plethora of different methodologies out there, such as Waterfall, Scrum, Kanban and Crystal. From our experience across multiple projects with multiple teams and multiple companies across the globe, the most common now are those that fall under the umbrella of agile, with some using the phrase 'agile' to refer directly to their process rather than to the group as a whole.

But there is one underlying set of ideas that should form the bedrock of any process that a company uses: the 'agile manifesto'. This was initially developed by software engineers, but it can be applied to any project or industry. There are four values and 12 guiding principles that any process should follow in order to be considered agile; let's look at these now.

FOUR AGILE VALUES

1. **Individuals and interactions** over processes and tools.

2. **Working software** over comprehensive documentation.

3. **Customer collaboration** over contract negotiation.

4. **Responding to change** over following a plan.

With each of these values, it should be noted that it's not that the item on the right isn't valuable – it is (yes, including documentation for any developers reading this). It is simply that the item on the left is valued more highly.

In my opinion, the top two values should be valued the most highly: no matter the methodology chosen, the most important thing will always be the individuals who are going to be following it and their interactions, and the main output should always be the software itself. By valuing the people over a rigid process, the process can be flexed to best serve the needs of the team using it. This is exemplified by the servant leadership style many project managers use, and should help the team to develop software in a collaborative style that has the flexibility to respond to any changes that may come down the line from the iterative feedback loop of the build–measure–learn cycle.

12 AGILE PRINCIPLES

The 12 principles of the agile manifesto help to reinforce the four values and build on them:

1. Our highest priority is to satisfy the customer through early and continuous delivery of valuable software.

2. Welcome changing requirements, even late in development. Agile processes harness change for the customer's competitive advantage.

3. Deliver working software frequently, from a couple of weeks to a couple of months, with a preference to the shorter timescale.

4. Business people and developers must work together daily throughout the project.

5. Build projects around motivated individuals. Give them the environment and support they need, and trust them to get the job done.

6. The most efficient and effective method of conveying information to and within a development team is face-to-face conversation.

7. Working software is the primary measure of progress.

8. Agile processes promote sustainable development. The sponsors, developers and users should be able to maintain a constant pace indefinitely.

9. Continuous attention to technical excellence and good design enhances agility.

10. Simplicity – the art of maximising the amount of work not done – is essential.

11. The best architectures, requirements and designs emerge from self-organising teams.

12. At regular intervals, the team reflects on how to become more effective, then tunes and adjusts its behaviour accordingly.

There are numerous resources that can help to break down these 12 principles in more detail; however, in short, as mentioned above, they help to reinforce and embellish the four agile values to guide teams in developing their own processes while retaining the core of what makes agile methodologies so popular amongst development companies.

INCEPTION, BUILD AND HANDOVER

So, initial prototyping and modelling? Check.

Process decided and agreed as a team with the client? Check.

A wise colleague once described these to me as the equivalent of the pre-flight checks on a flight. After this there are only three stages left: take-off, cruising altitude and landing. These can be mapped to the remaining stages of the project: inception, build and handover.

INCEPTION

The inception is a summation of all the work already done, starting from the Design Sprint, and incorporating that into a single vision that the development team can get behind.

Usually one of the more difficult parts of this is deciding on the scope of the project. With all the work done before, and with spirits high at the beginning of the project, it is often hard to then set restrictions on what the scope of an initial build or minimum viable product (MVP) should be. There has to be a balance between timescales, scope and budget. This is often difficult to strike, and numerous exercises can help to try to establish what the highest priority is.

Equally, at this point, there may be a need to take on board the technical needs of the product. This is sometimes difficult as non-technical product owners may not be aware of why these are needed, and so assign them a lower priority than customer-facing features. Negotiating this successfully often sets the tone of the project and can really get things off to a strong start.

There are numerous other activities in inception that can be carried out, and there are lots of good resources and blogs out there that can guide you through running a successful inception and kicking your project off on the right foot. With a successful take-off, we've reached cruising altitude and it's time for the build phase.

BUILD

'We're now cruising at 30,000ft. You may now unfasten your seatbelt and wander around the cabin...'

If only it was that straightforward! From a process perspective, this phase is all about executing the plan you've put in place, enabling and directing the team to develop the product. However, as with a flight, there can be turbulence and course corrections; but if you're following the agile principles and an appropriate methodology, these should give you all the help you need to get over any hurdles.

So let's now look at the pros and cons of two of the main agile methodologies used in software development – Scrum and Kanban – and how they operate to help the development team. They both work in an iterative manner, but have some key differences which we can explore below.

Scrum

Scrum is one of the most popular agile methodologies, to the extent that some of its terminologies have become synonymous with agile. The basis of Scrum is working through cycles known as sprints.

Sprints themselves are just allotted periods of time ranging from one week to four weeks. They contain a preset series of ceremonies, beginning with a team planning session to assess the scope of the sprint. This is done with the client or stakeholders, and assesses the priorities of the project, alongside the size and scope of the individual tasks (known as 'user stories'). The selected stories are then taken out of the product backlog, put into the sprint backlog, and form the majority of the work that the development team will be focusing on for this sprint.

There are scheduled daily stand-ups which allow the team to update everyone on progress made and predicted progress that day. It provides a chance for the product owner to understand the process and the complexities, and if anything is blocking progress it allows the team to rally round and remove the block.

Then there are two ceremonies to close out the sprint: the 'showcase' and the 'retrospective'. At the showcase, stakeholders are invited to view the progress made in the sprint, which should be demonstrated from a live or client-accessible environment. This allows you to continue the work done early in the Design Sprint and test the build with real users, which is an invaluable source of information. The suggestions and changes here can be built into future iterations. It's always good practice to keep a log of any of these changes for reference just in case you need them further down the line. Then, finally, in the retrospective, the sprint can be assessed as to its success, and you can discuss ways to improve and put in place a new implementation plan.

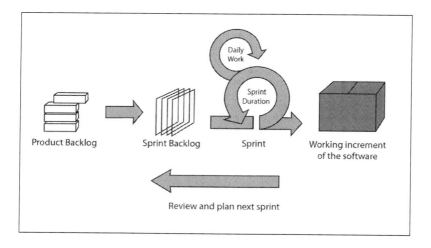

Kanban

Kanban takes a very similar approach to Scrum and has many of the same ceremonies in terms of daily stand-ups and retrospectives. The key difference between them is that where Scrum relies on sprints and timescales, Kanban sets no such timescales and instead works on a continually evolving priority backlog, with developers taking the highest priority ticket from the top of the backlog. Where Scrum plans and showcases at a sprint level, Kanban plans and showcases at an individual story level, although it still holds a retrospective on a regular basis to continue to refine processes and reflect on what has been achieved.

Both methodologies have incredible merits and improve efficiencies in the software development process. They can offer deep insights, and, as ever, there are a lot of resources available to help you understand the setups and tools for running Kanban or Scrum boards physically or virtually.

Most people will develop a preference for either one or the other methodology, but both have their pros and cons; I've also known teams that have transitioned between the methodologies depending on their circumstances. I initially cut my teeth in project management learning Scrum, but since then have used both over the years. Scrum works well when clients and product owners need structure and don't have the time to be continually available for planning individual user stories. Kanban, in contrast, offers a much greater level of flexibility in terms of what developers can pick up, and doesn't have the same level of strictness on timescales.

No matter what methodology you choose, the important thing is to build, test, learn and iterate – **always** – and wherever possible test products with real users to improve feedback quality and ensure that what is produced best matches the needs of the users.

And now the destination comes into view, there's only one last thing to do. We've got to land this bird.

HANDOVER

So, you've tested the prototype, you've decided on an MVP scope, and you've built a product and been iteratively testing it with real users. Now it's time for the final hurdle on the project: the handover. Depending on how the project has progressed, the landing can be either easy or more difficult.

For the purposes of this chapter, we'll be essentially describing to you the checklist of what needs to be done for a handover to be considered complete, and to give yourself the best chance of handing over a project successfully, whether that be to external clients or other internal teams.

First and most important is to have **working** software. Throughout the project, the product owner and stakeholders should have had access to the product, so not much here should be a surprise. The demonstration of the software should be end-to-end and showcase as many features as possible. This gives the truest example of what the team has developed and shows the hard work that has gone into development. It almost goes without saying that this should be rehearsed beforehand.

Second, yes it's that dreaded word, documentation. Whether it be the feature set with changelogs or user guides or technical documents, the documentation is important. This can include items such as shared exports of boards and statistics as well. Some of this may need to be done securely and outside of a handover session, for example when sharing code repositories, passwords or technical data. As such, this sort of handover may need multiple sessions and should be organised in advance so that all the relevant people are available for their sessions. All of these forms of documentation complement the working software well and will help any future developers or stakeholders understand the product and why certain decisions were made in development.

Finally, ask yourself one last question: 'Is there any reason the client won't sign off the project or pay the final invoice?' If the answer is yes, plug the gap (if it is reasonable to do so) so that the sign-off process is easy, or at least make sure to understand potential objections to the project being signed off and be prepared to deal with them.

With that, it's just a case of doing the grand demo and the handover sessions, raising your final invoice and getting the final sign-off... sounds easy, right? Of course, along the way there will always be bumps and things will not go according to plan, but hopefully this quick guide will assist you to reduce the number and impact of such issues.

TAKEAWAYS

- Plan out your prototype.

- Get out of the building to test it.

- Build, measure, test, learn, repeat.

- Pick an appropriate process.

- Iterate on your process, not just your product.

- Prepare your handover.

11

THE IMPORTANCE OF CULTURE

GUY REMOND

INTRODUCTION

In the following chapter, we'll discuss the history of Cake Solutions and how important our expert content generation was for marketing. Eventually, we embedded this ethos into our culture, but the reality is that we stumbled more or less by accident into realising how important culture is in a company, and how a well-structured cultural platform can be the foundation to drive growth in an organisation.

During a six-month period of research and development, our senior engineer Jan began to blog about his exploits and talk about his experiments on the Spring Framework in talks at user groups and conferences. He began to generate a following. This was the 'A-hah!' moment. We realised that the blogs and the talks were resulting in Jan building his own personal brand and by default that of Cake.

Our strategy now began to shift focus so that we were giving Jan as much time as we could afford in order to continue down the path of expert content generation and sharing with the tech community. Cake grew on the back of the sales either generated by referrals or by companies who required help reaching out to us because they had heard about us through Jan's activities.

Expert content generation became the backbone of our culture. We then began to look at the other facets of culture, so we not only generated sales but we generated interest from potential employees wanting to work for a company that specialised in this tech space, and we made the company 'sticky' so no one wanted to leave. We never used a recruiter to help us hire permanent members of the team; our applicants were engineers who were genuinely interested in the technologies we specialised in. Our retention rate was extremely high with very few people leaving and many new talented engineers joining the company for all the right reasons.

Our strategy to develop our culture over the next few years was fundamental to our success. We will discuss expert content generation in the next chapter, so this chapter will look at the other areas we purposefully developed in building a cultural platform that would provide the foundation for high growth and ultimately led to Cake being acquired.

PEOPLE

Hiring the right people means looking at candidates' commitment and potential contribution to your organisation's overall vision and strategy, and their ability to continually improve and innovate within their roles so that they provide direction and leadership in their area of expertise rather than waiting to receive it.

Once you have begun to build a culture, you will find that hiring the right people becomes easier. Firstly, having a voice and presence in your community means that candidates are more likely to seek you out. If they've read your blog posts and listened to your podcast, they have some understanding of what you are about, the technologies you specialise in, and the experts that they may be working with. This in itself is a filter: the quality and relevance of applications automatically improve because of this.

I also think it is incredibly important that your culture is discussed during the interview process. An interview is about you selling your company to the interviewee as much as it is about the interviewee selling themselves to you, and your culture is fundamental to this – both you and they have to be sure they'll be a good fit in the culture of your company. Testing the interviewee's technical skills and discussing your culture will help you both make a much more informed decision as to whether the interviewee would be a good fit in your company.

ENVIRONMENT

One of the most appreciated and profitable things you can do when it comes to culture is to create a collaborative atmosphere in your office(s). Make it comfortable and easy for people to get together and have chats and brainstorm. People need to communicate, and if you want your team to be creative, take more ownership and be more accountable; they need the freedom to communicate with their co-workers, build trust, innovate and make decisions together.

I always put a lot of thought into designing any new office space during my time at Cake, and now at thestartupfactory.tech, based on the ideas outlined above. With each new space, I have tried to up my game and improve on the last.

This all started when we first rented a much larger office space for the growing team at Cake. The office was filled with dated 1980s MFI-type furniture – for anyone under the age of 40 you may need to Google that reference! It was a blank canvas and came at a time when we were first beginning to understand the importance of culture. We didn't have the money to hire a design company, and in some ways, I'm glad we didn't. It allowed us to think carefully about how we used the space so it supported our ideas on culture.

I don't have space in this chapter to talk about each concept in detail. However, in short, we implemented the following ideas: each engineer had plenty of space to work; there were many meeting areas in relation to the space we had; every meeting area had a branded drywipe board; the coffee shop and board room had a table you could draw on; you could work from a sofa, your desk, a spare meeting room or a standing desk; we had wall and glass graphics around the office with relevant images, such as code, talking points, quotes, etc.; the interior walls were modern glass partitions with frosted privacy bands; we subtly branded areas of the office as a subliminal reinforcement of the company brand that hopefully everyone was proud to work for – and the list goes on.

In essence, I always aim to offer my team as comfortable, relaxing, inspiring and creative a space as I can that reflects the culture of the company.

TOOLS AND RESOURCES

It can be very easy for business owners to underestimate the importance of giving their team the best possible resources and tools they need to do their jobs. Of course, being the founder of a technology company with a focus on design and innovation, you should have the most up-to-date software and hardware. There are now thousands of different platforms for all different business functions, and utilising the right ones for your business and your teams can increase and improve communication, efficiency and the quality of the service your clients receive.

We advise that you invest in technology: for example, having all equipment be less than three years old ensures that your team can work efficiently and run processor/memory intensive operations quickly. You could also use software-as-a-service (SaaS) offerings that allow your team to work efficiently from anywhere using the best technology available. At Cake we had no servers in our office from 2010, preferring the flexibility, ease and often cost savings that SaaS services offered.

Thinking about tools and resources also doesn't necessarily mean technology. It could mean giving your team access to coaching and development opportunities, events, books and technical resources.

One such policy at Cake that reflected our culture of continual improvement was giving anyone who wanted a book the ability to order it – they didn't need authorisation, they just asked the admin team to request it, and once they'd read it they would leave it in our library for everyone to benefit from.

'Lunch and Learns' were another key element of what we did. Many members of the team would present their views and knowledge on a particular technology to the rest of the team at lunchtime. This allowed them to hone their presentation skills and allowed the team to benefit from their expertise. We always provided food and drink as a way to facilitate these events.

Another example was that, whenever possible, we organised world-renowned experts to visit the office and do a talk in their specialist area – this really boosted the morale of the team. They had the opportunity to listen to their heroes talk!

In summary, providing your team with the right tools and resources helps to develop a culture of continual improvement – of the team themselves and of performance.

PERKS AND BENEFITS

Normally when people discuss perks and benefits it is in relation to healthcare, dental care, all the standard stuff. I take a different view. I see perks and benefits as things we can offer that add to our culture and ethos. Health, fitness and personal development are central to vibrant culture.

Healthcare insurance, for example, looks to reactively solve an issue that has already occurred. I prefer to take a proactive approach and offer gym memberships to all of my team in an effort to keep them healthy. In another example, one of our team suggested having fresh fruit available for people to help themselves to – a great idea, and it was done immediately.

A real benefit of working for Cake was our philosophy of continual personal development. We actively encouraged personal improvement in all of our strategies and thinking, from the creative and collaborative environment of the office to our open policy on ordering books. Everybody who worked for Cake improved their technical knowledge and their softer skills at pace because of the environment and ethos.

I believe we also had a flexible way of working that was different to most but was a real benefit to the team. Most companies seem to offer traditional working arrangements where workers come in at a set time and go home at a set time, or they offer full flexi-time which is almost the polar opposite. We took the view that we needed to provide flexibility whilst leveraging the undoubted benefits of working in a team in the same physical location.

If anyone ever needed to work from home for a day or two to be around for a delivery, go to the dentist, look after children etc., they just arranged it with their team lead. But the majority of the time was spent together in the office: I have no doubt that teams working in the same physical location benefit in the form of social contact and the ability to tap someone on the shoulder and work with them in person to solve a problem.

Essentially, try to think carefully about what perks and benefits you could offer, and don't just follow the route most corporates take. This approach gives you a competitive edge and is far more beneficial to your team.

PERSONAL BEHAVIOURAL DEVELOPMENT

Personal behavioural development is simply the combination of some of the ideas I have already discussed in this chapter: from the cultural thinking behind the environment to encourage those who want to build a personal brand, to engineers being encouraged to give presentations and speak directly with clients rather than being shielded from this. It's about improving not only in technical skills, which for most engineers is the number one priority, but in all the relevant areas. In my view, for example, soft skills development is also really important. To make the most of their technical skills, engineers need to understand how to communicate and interact with others effectively.

Personal behavioural development was baked into the Cake culture and is something we are developing at thestartupfactory.tech as well.

TECHNICAL IMPROVEMENT

Technical improvement is crucial in any company with technical teams. Make sure that your strategy is well thought out rather than ad hoc and haphazard.

We have already touched on a number of ways that we developed technical improvement at Cake in this chapter: the ability to order books at will as one method of learning; the Lunch and Learns that we held almost weekly; the experts we invited to the office who presented their latest ideas to the team; the conferences and user groups that team members attended and talked at; and the blog writing (between us we wrote over 700 blogs in a seven-year period). In addition, each team purposefully had a mix of experience, which meant that there was always someone to learn from in a continual cycle of improvement.

The projects we worked on in the main were complex and interesting. They often pushed the technical capabilities of the team. We strongly believed that one of the best ways of learning was to work in an experienced team trying to solve difficult technical issues. This was strategic: we aimed to work on this type of project whenever commercially possible.

Technical improvement was baked into our culture and was one of the main reasons why we had such a high retention rate.

COMMUNICATION

Part of any strategy to have a fully engaged team is regular communication from the leadership. Over the years, as Cake grew so did our communication strategy. We moved from a small team where communication was easy and constant, to a team of over 70 where we needed a proper process to lead regular communications. We embedded it in our culture.

The leadership team evolved its communication strategy to include quarterly company updates, monthly company update newsletters and ad hoc meetings to deal with specific events. It is so important that the team are made aware of the great stuff happening in the company, as well as (up to a point) some of the not-so-good things. This engenders a feeling of belonging: sharing the joy of a significant commercial win, a successful conference, a successful product demo to a client. It also draws attention to any issues in the business that need to be solved.

And as part of the technical process, the teams applied rigorous agile and lean practices which took care of project communication. This should be ingrained into your team's process, too.

TAKEAWAYS

- Building a cultural platform is one of the most important factors in setting your company up for high growth, hiring incredible people and generating high profit margins that can be reinvested into continued growth.

- A culture of continuous learning and development can be established using several different strategies, such as a carefully considered setup of the office environment, or a policy of paying for team members to attend and present at conferences.

- Culture makes you stand out from your competitors; if you have a great culture, clients will notice and will often want to emulate it. A strong culture is often the main reason another company hears about yours, falls in love with it, and perhaps eventually wants to acquire it.

PART 3

IN IT
FOR THE
LONG
HAUL

12

MARKETING ON A SHOESTRING

GUY REMOND

INTRODUCTION

Marketing is going through a fundamental change at the moment and has been since the arrival of blogging and social media platforms. Marketing for most organisations is moving online and away from the traditional mediums that were used for so many years. The issue is that there are so many opportunities to spend your hard-earned marketing budget online it can be difficult to know where to start.

MARKETING AT CAKE

At Cake, we took a very different and, in the end, a very deliberate approach to promoting the company. One of the most important aspects that drove our culture was our senior engineer Jan embarking on research and development projects which he blogged about and spoke about at conferences, resulting in him building a personal brand. We already understood the importance of expert content generation from the benefits that came our way off the back of co-authoring or authoring a number of books in the early days of the company. These books included *Pro Jakarta Struts* (2004), *Pro Visual Studio .NET* (2004), and the two bestselling *Pro Spring* books (2005 and 2008).

The interest Jan was generating with his blogs and talks was not just increasing our notoriety; it was generating sales. In fact, a blog on how Jan had used machine learning in one of his projects caught the attention of a company in the US from the automotive sector. They quickly became one of our biggest clients at that time. We began to attract the interest of quite a number of big companies in the UK, UAE and US working on major projects, the majority of which were seven-figure deals.

As well as generating direct interest, the blogs, user group talks, open source projects and conference presentations caught the attention of the companies who were developing the technologies we were evangelising about. This led to us forming strong partnerships with a number of them, including Lightbend and DataStax. It was a marriage made in heaven: we genuinely believed in their products and naturally evangelised about them when talking about what we were up to.

We also gave these technologies commercial credibility; we were using them to build applications that needed to scale in a big way, perform well and deal with huge amounts of data in a cloud environment with big-name companies. The huge benefit for us was being associated with the ultimate expert in the technologies we specialised in, and they became a rich source of referrals. It was a genuine win-win where no money exchanged hands – the best type of partnership.

Right from the outset of Jan generating expert content derived from his experiments, we saw the positive effect that had on the company. He was building a personal brand which benefited the company by association. To speak with or work with Jan, companies had to approach Cake. We then, very deliberately, started to encourage the whole team to multiply the expert content effect and build their own personal brands. By multiplying our voice in the technical community, we were reaching more and more potential clients and, as a nice strategic by-product, many more potential employees.

THE BENEFIT OF CREATING
PERSONAL BRANDS

Not everybody in your company will want to put themselves out there in this way, but many do, and most actually saw it as one of the huge benefits of working at Cake. In the end, I suspect we had at least 50% of the company contributing in some way on a reasonably regular basis, either through a blog, a user group talk, a conference talk or contributing code that we had written to the open source community.

There are real benefits for the employees as well: building a personal brand in the technical community of the technologies they specialise in is the best and probably the only CV they will ever need if they ever did want to leave Cake. I like to think that everyone who joined Cake did so because they really wanted to work using the technologies we specialised in, and also because our culture of encouraging them to talk about their passions was of real benefit to the team. It led to further learning and staying ahead of what was happening in their area of expertise.

This kind of culture also helps develop the soft skills of the employees. I saw engineers arrive shy and introverted, and steadily over time develop into team leads who communicated with and influenced our clients on a daily basis. This was down to the effort and determination of the team members themselves and the culture at Cake. If the team member wanted to have a voice in the technical community, by making the most of the platform (in a reputational sense) Cake had built, they could do that. It might start with them writing a blog, then presenting at a 'Lunch and Learn', before moving on to speak at user groups and conferences as their confidence increased. Again, another win–win.

It takes effort to develop a culture that encourages this type of behaviour. Some team members have to be coaxed out of their comfort zone, but when this happens they love the opportunity presented to them. Some never will, which is fine. They may just want to concentrate on their technical development but do it quietly.

SUPPORT YOUR TEAM

The reputation of Cake as a very competent technical organisation was built by the hard work and talent of the original team members contributing to the personal brand concept. They put the company on the map and created the platform which other developers could benefit from later, in that being a Cake employee would guarantee them a spot to present at a conference, or immediately give their blog a head start. Their expert content generation continued to build their own brand and the company's reputation, and we supported them in doing so.

To truly support your team to build personal brands, you have to give them some time to do it. It's a fine balance to be able to offer this as well as ensure you get client work done to make the profit that allows for this kind of opportunity. In fact, blogs and presentations were usually created during a mix of both work time and personal time.

It can also cost more than time to support these activities; when a team member has a talk accepted at a conference the costs can add up: hotels, travel (often flights), food, etc. However, the benefits to the organisation can be huge.

It is worth dealing here with a fear that many entrepreneurs have when encouraging their engineering team to build a personal brand: recruiters! Unfortunately, recruiters trying to poach your talent are a fact of life and will be an issue for you with or without your engineers building their personal brand. In my view, the recruiters themselves are not the issue when it comes to staff leaving: the issue actually lies with the companies who employ these great people.

The bottom line is that if you have invested in building a strong culture for your organisation it becomes very hard – if not impossible – for recruiters to poach your team. Why would anyone want to leave a company that specialises in their preferred technologies, invests in their training and personal development, gives them great tools to use and a lovely environment to work in? If you don't have that in place, losing your best engineers will always be a risk, with or without personal brand building, and with or without recruiters!

INVEST IN THE RIGHT MARKETING TECHNOLOGY

One other major benefit to Cake was that we didn't need a large marketing team: inbound leads were generated from the team building personal brands, which meant we didn't have to do much else. Plus the leads were pre-filtered: any company contacting us knew what we were about, what our areas of expertise were and how good we were thanks to the expert content.

The only function of marketing we needed to do in addition to the content was to make sure it was distributed across the internet effectively. After all, you can write lots of great blog posts, but if no one reads them, they have no marketing value! So we invested time and money into technology to help with this, specifically Hubspot, a modern marketing solution.

Hubspot had a blogging platform that we used, as well as hosting our website on the platform. This allowed us to efficiently distribute every piece of content the team produced across Twitter and LinkedIn over multiple accounts with the click of a button. In addition, we built up a decent-sized database of people interested in what we had to say and used a monthly email newsletter to promote the blogs and anything else happening in the business we thought they would be interested in. Everything worked together and, once set up, required very little effort to maintain.

More and more founders are realising how important producing and sharing expert content is to promote their company. This can be used in isolation or in conjunction with other marketing activities – the only other marketing channel we used at Cake was advertising on StackOverflow, a platform that software engineers use to ask a question or provide support to other engineers.

However you set things up, you need to stay on top of the new technologies and content channels as the landscape changes. For example, podcasts are becoming a more and more important method of sharing expertise. Back in the mid-2000s, podcasts were around but were not a mainstream method of distributing expert content, so we didn't use them at that point in time; however, things progress. Employing a strategy of building a strong culture and an ethos of building personal brands will get you noticed in all the right ways and improve your bottom line.

TAKEAWAYS

- Having your team members create personal brands is a win–win for both the company and for themselves.

- Personal brands are created through blog posts, books and conference presentations. Get the expertise in your company out there and watch as clients start coming directly to you.

- Support your team in this, while also making sure clients' work is getting done.

- Use the right technology to best distribute your expert content, or help your marketing effort in whatever way you need.

13

NOT JUST AN ACCOUNTANT

ELLIOT SMITH

INTRODUCTION

One of the first things startups and entrepreneurs are advised to do is to find a good accountant. But what constitutes a good accountant?

It goes without saying that a good accountant should excel in processing and reporting on accounting data, ensuring statutory compliance and ensuring company taxes are filed in good time. But shouldn't they also have the capability and experience needed to help business founders run, expand and eventually sell their business? It's the delivery of this extra dimension that differentiates a great accountant from the norm.

Despite having strong products, services and ideas, many businesses fail to reach their full potential simply because of poor financial management or a failure to bring in the required expertise at the right time. Having a good accountant can, quite simply, be the difference between failure and success.

In this chapter, I'm going to explain why having a sound financial strategy, supported by the right personnel, is so important to the success of a business. I'll also discuss the key considerations relating to the partnerships you'll need to build with different finance professionals along the way, each of whom will become an integral part of your growth plan and future success.

ACCOUNTING AT A STARTUP TECH BUSINESS

So, you've got a great idea and have formed a company, where do you go from here?

I think most entrepreneurs would acknowledge that accounting doesn't come naturally to them, which explains why it is an area that is often neglected during the early stages in the life of a business. Even those with experience of working with accountants previously may not want to spend their time focusing on this at the outset, and would rather prioritise product/service development, sales and marketing.

I'd go so far as to say that many entrepreneurs view their accountants as risk-averse individuals who prefer to run a business through a spreadsheet, always ready to throw up barriers designed to frustrate entrepreneurial thinking and their way of doing things. Conversely, many accountants view entrepreneurs as risk-takers who are unable to control the following of their gut instincts and are continually flying by the seat of their pants.

Adopting a more balanced view of these two positions creates a better environment for success, by recognising that both differing skill sets have a role to play and are both essential in order to take a business on a journey from formation to scale and sale.

In the early stages of any tech business, it's likely that the founder's primary focus will be on the creation of a minimum viable product, finding the right tech partner, and the development of an investment deck suitable for raising funds. It's unlikely that they are lying awake at night worrying about current and future accountancy issues. That's because it's just not viewed as a priority. In fact, it's probably viewed as an unnecessary, time-consuming and costly evil.

However, even in the very early stages of any business, you are likely to face many financial challenges, and there's a good chance you will be exposed to having to manage the day-to-day financial transactions yourself, handling cashflow problems, struggling to raise finance and managing your tax affairs correctly and compliantly. Is it a realistic expectation for you to manage all the financial aspects of the new business on your own?

The obvious solution is to hire an accountant; but what sort of accountant is going to be best for your business's development, both now and in the future?

THE GATEKEEPER: TRADITIONAL ACCOUNTANT

Typically, the primary role of an accountant has been viewed as somebody who manages and oversees a company's finance function, and is responsible for the transaction processing in a company and reporting on those transactions. Their focus is often described as reactive, compliance-led and emotionally detached. Personally, I would describe it more as a basic customer/supplier relationship rather than a partnership.

The vast majority of startups select their accountant based on cost and expect little more than a compliance-led service and occasional advice on an ad hoc basis, along with the annual preparation of year-end accounts and tax returns. And that's pretty much all they get. Little input into the business is given, bar a set of accounts that get filed away and instruction on what taxes are due and when.

Now there's nothing wrong with this approach, and many firms function well with the gatekeeper relationship because everybody understands it and it works. However, the truth is that a gatekeeper accountant will probably never challenge or question your strategy, i.e. what you are doing, why you are doing it, or offer an opinion. They will not concern themselves with the future development and success of the company, as this is seen as falling outside the scope of their services and engagement. Ultimately, they'd see that as the responsibility of the board and will not advise on this side of the business unless specifically asked to do so.

The compliance side of accountancy is a valued, necessary service, and a gatekeeper accountant relationship will be perfectly adequate if you are a micro, lifestyle company with little or no ambition to expand beyond this. However, if you are entrepreneurial with aspirations of high growth, you will definitely benefit from a much closer relationship with your accountant, where you receive the high level of day-to-day support you'll need to help you strategise, manage, expand and eventually sell your business.

THE GUARDIAN: MODERN ACCOUNTANT

The role of accountant has changed dramatically over the past decade, with many firms now providing more specialist advisory-based services, whilst being more receptive to collaboration and embracing the entrepreneurial spirit.

Advances in technology have been a key driver behind these changes, with it now being far easier for businesses to process data and obtain an insight into financial performance through software and apps. Every aspect of a business's key financial information can now be made available in real time to assist day-to-day decision-making, financial reporting and compliance thanks to modern tech, and this has led to modern accountants developing a wider range of capabilities. This includes technical, analytical and business skills, which enable them to offer support far beyond their core financial expertise. They are no longer viewed just as bean counters but as potential strategic partners, bringing a range of practical, financial and commercial knowledge to the table.

In addition to offering the traditional gatekeeper services, a modern accountant will act as a guardian, using their experience and expertise to advise and guide you through your business journey, their involvement growing with the business and assisting with all matters financial, often going above and beyond what is asked of them. As part of their core services, particular emphasis will be placed on how to improve finances, deal with risk and reduce tax.

For instance, they may prepare monthly or quarterly management accounts and present them to the board, providing an insight into the intricacies that lie behind the financial performance of the business and the commercial considerations that drive them. Without a doubt, this level of support will help you make sound decisions about the direction of the business and its future.

For businesses that are looking to scale up quickly, it is important to have a modern accountant whose role can grow with your needs and support you at varying stages in your journey. Not all startups will be equipped to do this, and costs may be a barrier to bringing in higher levels of expertise, particularly in the early stages of a business. Nonetheless, it's important to find the right balance between compliance- and advisory-based support to facilitate and assist with growth.

THE STRATEGIST: FINANCE DIRECTOR

Accountants will generally spend the majority of their time forecasting, budgeting and reporting, which may not be seen as adding value or being integral to the strategy of a company. A finance director, however, will fulfil much of the required strategic finance partner role, which, as you will see, will bring medium- to long-term value to your company.

In addition to having a complete working knowledge of the company's financial position, a finance director will be briefed in and assist with the development of the company's vision and its core objectives. They will have a full understanding of all areas of the business, not just its financial affairs, which will allow them to advise on the balance between risk, opportunities and reward. As part of your senior team, a good finance director will help the board develop a clear, long-term business growth plan, along with a supporting financial strategy.

Working in collaboration with your finance director, you would look to implement a management framework and process capable of delivering the growth plan, recruit a senior team and improve the levels of professionalism within the business. In addition to their financial expertise, as part of their core attributes they will be able to:

- Think strategically and commercially.

- Visualise the future of the company.

- Understand profit drivers.

- Turn financial data into insightful and meaningful reports.

- Be more interested in affecting the future than reporting on the past.

- Challenge and support the board.

- Influence and work with people who drive performance, i.e. in sales, marketing and operations.

Historically, financial personnel were only seen as the financial custodians of a company, and in many circumstances that is still the case. However, nowadays, forward-thinking businesses recognise the value of seeing their finance personnel more like partners, able to participate in the development of the company's vision, whilst encouraging them to focus on strategic value-added services, rather than data processing and reporting. The right finance team will instil a positive finance mindset throughout a business that will help other areas to perform better which, in turn, will be a catalyst for growth.

MY JOURNEY

I started my career at what I would refer to as a typical gatekeeper firm of accountants. All day every day was spent churning out sets of accounts, which once drafted were passed to the head accountant. There was very little engagement with clients or other personnel within the firm, and the general culture running through that business was to do nothing more than what we were engaged to do.

After three years, I was becoming quite disillusioned with this way of approaching things and was continually thinking there must be more to accountancy than this. I decided to make a move to industry, where I joined an entrepreneurial business to lead their finance team. Shortly after joining, the founder began to sound me out on a variety of financial and other business-related items on a regular basis.

At last I was asked for an opinion and actively encouraged to give one.

I was still gaining experience at this stage, but this new challenge was something that I thoroughly relished. I could see a bright future in this way of doing things because my opinion was being valued. My input was having a positive effect across the business and I was now being viewed as a partner rather than just another member of the finance team.

A return to practice followed, where I joined a young ambitious firm as an equity partner. I subsequently spent the next 10 years here, assisting with developing the practice into a modern accountancy firm.

As well as being an accountant, the founder was very entrepreneurial and actively encouraged us to collaborate with our clients. Together we decided the time was right to go for high growth. By using the latest technology, offering new products/services and going above and beyond what was asked of us, we were able to build some very strong client relationships. On reflection, I suppose the main difference from my previous experience in practice was that I was now being proactive rather than reactive.

With this new approach we were able to exploit a gap in the market. We started to offer an advanced level of collaborative financial support to businesses with great potential that were still too young in their development to warrant an internal finance department or finance director of their own.

As part of this role, I subsequently started to work with Cake Solutions, where I met and worked alongside my co-authors Guy Remond (the founder) and Ian Brookes (a non-exec). These two individuals were to become a big part of my personal and professional journey and development over the coming years.

I became their accountant at a very exciting time in Cake's development, when they had made the decision to aim for high growth. It was during this period that I became integral to developing Cake's financial strategy. Along the way, I became their part-time finance director and was involved in all major decisions relating to finance which, as you can imagine, covered pretty much every aspect of the business. I attended the monthly board meetings and briefed the board on the company's finances, whilst having a continual involvement in Cake's growth plans by setting out exactly what targets we wanted to achieve, how we were going to deliver them and reporting on the results.

Having the opportunity to share my opinion and being involved in making those decisions, I became an integral part of the management team and I am in no doubt that this was a really important factor in the successful development of the company, having a particularly big impact on Cake's ability to sustain high growth over a relatively short period of time.

One of the most important things I've learnt in my years in the industry is that entrepreneurial founders really excel when they have the freedom to do what they're best at, safe in the knowledge that their finance personnel are supportive, proactive and have the capacity to be much more than a bean counter. And, whilst financial personnel do not necessarily drive performance, they can certainly have a big influence on it.

WHAT IS THERE TO BE GAINED FROM ALL OF THIS?

Most founders realise they will need support to achieve their objectives, and that developing strategic partnerships with the right people at the right time is often the key to success. Founders need time and freedom to be creative, so they can drive the business forward using their core expertise. So, delegating the company's finance function and strategy will give them more time to be creative, and makes complete sense.

I'm a great believer in inviting key employees, customers and suppliers to adopt a company's ethos and culture, because they could all be described as stakeholders, partners who have a hand in the potential success of a business. The actual type of relationship doesn't really matter, be it an employee, a contractor, a board advisor or a non-exec director, because these stakeholders should all be considered valued members of the team.

With the required support and expertise in your team, you'll once again have the time and energy to apply your focus towards working on the business, rather than in the business.

AS A BUSINESS GROWS, ITS NEEDS CHANGE TOO

Whatever stage your business is at, it is important for a scaling business to have a forward-thinking finance partner that is able and willing to challenge your thinking. Those finance partners with the right attributes will grow with the business and continue to offer the full spectrum of commercial and financial support as and when your company needs it.

However, there may be instances where, for whatever reason, you outgrow your current finance partner, or they are no longer the right fit in the team. As soon as it becomes apparent that you are in need of a new finance partner, you should determine the level of support you now require. Involve other team members in the recruitment process and seek referrals from other successful entrepreneurs.

Depending on the size of your business, you may wish to consider employing an internal finance director in addition to an external accountant. This could be a flexible arrangement on a part-time and/or an outsourced basis, whichever is best to suit the needs of the business at that particular point in time. And, from experience, I'd say it's never too early to start thinking about engaging with someone who has an opinion on your company, what you're doing and why you are doing it.

Initially, this might be as a sounding board for a few hours a week or month, but even at this level it will add a lot of value to the business, its strategy, your thinking and direction. Evidence suggests that entrepreneurs and their finance partners should be able to achieve sustained growth faster when they work together collaboratively with a shared vision.

LOOKING AHEAD

In the future, finance is going to become even more automated, with data processing, forecasting, budgeting and reporting likely to be done by artificial intelligence (AI) in the coming years. As AI becomes more established, the role of the traditional accountant – and to a lesser extent the modern accountant – will be less in demand, with some of their current core service offerings becoming obsolete and of little value. I can see a time when the traditional role of an accountant will be redundant.

Instead, a new breed of commercially focused, financial strategists will evolve, perfectly suited to the new role, bringing with them experience from all areas of the business world; these new financial strategists will be far more valuable to businesses than a traditional accountant.

TAKEAWAYS

- Startups often face financial challenges; delegating the financials to someone who understands them better and is more engaged with them than you are likely to be is sensible.

- There are three types of accountant: the traditional accountant, whose focus is on reporting and accounts, and is generally seen as reactive, compliance-led and emotionally detached; the modern accountant, who in addition offers specialist advisory services and support beyond their core finance skills; and the finance director, who is fully embedded in the business and is a key partner, challenging the founder's thinking and proactively influencing decisions within the company.

- Your business's needs may well change as it grows; be prepared and willing to change up your choice of accountant depending on what you require.

- In the future, AI will be able to take over the majority of functions of the traditional accountant, so be aware of this and look for the value-added services offered by a modern accountant or finance director instead.

14

FINANCIAL ADVICE

SIMON BOOTH

INTRODUCTION

In 1995 I landed my dream job. Overnight I doubled my earnings and would be setting up a brand-new high-net-worth financial planning division for a large UK insurer. The company was using cutting-edge financial planning techniques brought in from the US, and my experience and examination success made me the perfect candidate for the job.

For two years I worked myself into the ground: we built up a team of 75 and were the top performing branch in the company. And then it started to go wrong. The dream job suddenly turned into a nightmare. It was obvious what the problem was, but the senior management of the company refused to acknowledge the reality and were driving what could have been an exceptionally successful business into a brick wall.

The experience gained at the insurer had been fantastic. My eyes had been opened to a new way of doing financial planning with wealthy clients that was the way forward. Unfortunately, it was run by a large company who had no idea of how to run a dynamic business. Worse than that, the company did not have the right financial products available for the high-net-worth market they had targeted, and were now asking us as managers to push our advisors to invest in investments that were not suitable for them, because those were the only plans they had available.

So, at the end of 1997, I found myself sitting in my beautiful office overlooking the basin at Salford Quays in Manchester wondering what to do. There was only one answer. I had to do it myself. My father had been a business owner and it had always been my ambition to emulate him.

And so, on 16 February 1998, my new business started; 23 years on and I am still here. However, the journey began in an inauspicious way. I had intended to go into business with one of my colleagues, but she got cold feet and dropped out at the last moment. As I looked for premises it quickly became apparent that my naivety about how to set up a business was going to mean everything was a process of trial and error. Unfortunately, trial and error meant wasting significant amounts of money – a luxury that few budding business owners have in the beginning.

Eventually I opened an office at 92 Water Lane in Wilmslow for business and off I went. My offices were almost opposite the Aston Martin garage in Wilmslow and I was completely confident that my first order for an Aston Martin would be made before the end of the first year. I went for a test drive straight away so that I could work out the options that I would need. Suffice to say, I didn't need to trouble the Aston Martin garage again for quite some time, as the realities of running a business started to set in. But I have never looked back. Although I've had some significant issues along the way, there have been lots of wins too, and I would not have swapped the experience for anything.

The idea of this chapter is to give you some practical ideas about how to avoid the mistakes that I and many other business owners make when setting up. It's about how to run your finances in the best way and to make sure that you have the right elements covered at the right points in time. It also explains the need to get your personal finances as well as your business finances in order, and how this approach to finance ties in with the points Elliot covers earlier in this section of the book. It is, quite simply, all about the money.

THE SETUP

With the benefit of hindsight, I would have started my business later, because if I had stayed at the company for another 18 months, when they were closed down because of exactly the shortcomings that I had told them about, they would have given me a payoff of over £100,000 which would have funded everything.

As it was, I left at very short notice with what, in hindsight, was not the correct amount of money. Business owners are, by nature, optimistic people. You have to be, otherwise you would not bother. I like spreadsheets and had a whole range of them showing me what my expenditure would be, how much money would be flowing into the business and how long before it would start to flow in.

Within a short period of time it became obvious that my predictions had been far too optimistic. So, my first piece of advice is quite simple. Whatever turnover figure you think you are going to achieve in your first year, halve it. And double the length of time you think it is going to take to set your first business up. Although more of a guesstimation exercise, I have found this to be exceptionally accurate when dealing with other new business owners.

Getting your finances in order before setting up on your own is very important. Firstly, you need reserves because something will always go wrong. There will always be additional added expenses that you had no idea even existed. And everything takes far more time to set up than you could anticipate.

So, you need to be running a lean, mean, financial machine before setting up your business. This involves running through every single line of your bank account, deciding whether you are looking at a necessity or a luxury, and then making brutal decisions and slashing your spending.

Your finances are like a hamster wheel. The quicker the wheel spins, the faster it wants to go. Your job as a business owner is to get that hamster wheel spinning as slowly as possible to begin with so that it gives you a fighting chance of being successful.

Statistics show that 20% of businesses do not even make their first anniversary, and 60% have gone by the end of the third year. This is mainly because they never give themselves a fighting chance of making it right from the very beginning. This means you need to thoroughly understand not only your personal cashflow, but also the cashflow of the business.

This means sitting down and working on those business plans: they will never be exactly right, but they are a start and will show you the reality of running your own business. Reducing your own personal expenditure to a minimum will give you time, and that is exactly what you will need before success comes along.

The starting point must be the protection side of things. Rather like building a house, it is vitally important to ensure you have solid foundations. If you don't set up the right foundations you *may* get away with it, but then again you may not, and by the time you find out it will be too late to do anything about it.

First, it is vital that you get a will set up. Although this sounds very dull and boring, it is probably the most important thing that you, as a business owner, can provide for your family in the event of something going drastically wrong. Without it, it is highly unlikely that your assets will go to the right people at the right time.

You can do a will yourself by going down to WH Smith and picking up a will writing kit for about £20. However, there is only one thing worse than no will, and that is a poorly written will. My recommendation is to go to a good solicitor and get a professionally drafted will, which will cost you in the region of £200 to £400.

Second, you need to look at your protection planning. The important thing to remember here is that you are now your own employer. And who wants to work for a poor employer? Your job is to make sure that whatever happens to you, your income and family are secure moving forwards. This means looking at items such as life insurance, critical illness cover and even income protection. There are now ways to obtain tax relief on certain types of life cover and, once again, it makes good sense to get proper professional financial advice rather than trying to do it yourself.

Cashflow had not been something I was aware of in my previous employed positions with large companies. However, it quickly became obvious that cashflow was going to be key to ensuring the success of my business. Indeed, it became very clear very quickly that other more well-established and savvy business owners were far better at extracting money from me than I was at extracting money from them. This was a position that could not carry on indefinitely: it cost me dearly in the first few months, but it was a lesson that I have never forgotten and one that has served me well throughout my business life.

The next lesson is in bloody-mindedness. Working hard, working through the inevitable issues that will come along and proving to yourself that the experience and knowledge that you have will see you through. Running a business is reassuringly difficult – if it was easy then everybody would be doing it and would be successful. The fact it's reassuringly difficult means that only the best will survive, and only a few will get to reap the rich rewards of running their own business.

GROWING PAINS

Once you have made it through the first couple of years, this is typically when businesses start to grow. While in the first year your main concern was to make sure you had enough money for yourself, the emphasis has now moved on to making sure that you have enough money for both yourself and your team. Leveraging your knowledge and abilities is key to developing a successful business that you can sell on. That means employing staff and increasing both costs and turnover significantly.

However, this does not mean automatic financial success. And the main reason for this? Her Majesty's Revenue and Customs (HMRC). In the first year or two, tax is unlikely to be an issue. If you have employed a good accountant, then the first two years should be relatively tax-free. However, after that, HMRC can quite easily be your biggest bill each month.

It is important to get the right kind of accountant on board from the start. In my experience, there are two main types. Firstly, the ones who are agents of HMRC and who think their job is simply to calculate how much tax you should be sending off to them on an ongoing basis. Indeed, one of my clients had such an accountant who texted her while I was with her simply stating that she needed to pay £15,000 by the following day to avoid penalties. No explanation or mitigating strategies.

The second type of accountant is the one who works with you to ensure your tax bills are kept at the lowest level legally possible. However, these accountants are more expensive. You want to go with a reassuringly expensive accountant who has your best interests at heart, rather than simply hiring the cheapest one available.

Unfortunately, it can be difficult to work out in advance who fits these criteria. Ask other business owners who they use and what their experience was. A good accountant can make the difference between having a successful long-term business and not having a business at all.

You now need to look at your longer-term financial planning. This means getting hold of a good, holistic, independent financial advisor for a review of your current situation. And this is probably going to cost you a fee. An independent advisor is best because you want to know what is right for you, not simply be advised on what the advisor has in their briefcase. And holistic, because a lot of the advice is not going to be fee-generating – and it is often the non-fee-generating advice that is most important to you.

The idea is to make sure that you have the right preparations in place for when your business becomes significantly more successful in the future. This is when you need to start thinking about pensions for yourself (the government will have already made you provide pensions for your employees) and planning ahead. Individual savings accounts (ISAs) are also a great way of squirrelling money away for the longer term, whilst leaving the funds accessible if the need arises.

You need to make sure that those reserves are always growing. That hamster wheel is spinning ever faster. It is very tempting for new business owners to take that trip to the Aston Martin garage at this point, because they are mistaking turnover for profit and assuming that what has gone well to date will continue unabated into the future.

There have been three international crises that have hit my business in the last 20 years. The Dotcom crash of 2001 decimated financial markets and effectively reset economies for the next few years. This had a dampening effect on my business, but I got over it relatively quickly, because I only had a few staff and low overheads.

The banking crisis of 2008 caused real issues. We had been growing very quickly, had taken a significant number of new staff on board and were predicting even greater revenues in the following years. When the crisis hit, it did so with far greater force than anything that we had seen before. And the icing on the cake, of course, was that HMRC then popped up asking us for taxes relating to the previous years, even though our order book was now empty. We made decisions too slowly, too late and ineffectively. And it took a number of years to recover from that.

The Coronavirus pandemic, on the other hand, has had little effect on the business. This has in some part been down to luck; however, we were also determined not to be hit in the same way as before. This meant that we took action as soon as the scale of the crisis was known, we had significant reserves to fall back on, and as a mature business we had a large number of clients who we could continue to advise on an ongoing basis.

Running a business is about making the right decisions at the right time. They are often not easy decisions to make, but making them at the right time will ensure you feel better and that your business is more robust in the long term: it's the right thing to do.

WHAT'S YOUR NUMBER?

Once the initial growth spurt is over and you have successfully negotiated the pitfalls, it is now time to start thinking about an eventual sale of your business. The bottom line with the sale is that it's all about the money. It's your measure of success. It's what is going to give you and your family financial security. The freedom to do whatever it is that takes your fancy.

So the big question is, how much is enough? You need to know your number – the amount of money that you need to become financially independent. So just how much is enough? Stelios, the ex-EasyJet owner, allegedly once said that anything above £30 million is just for show, but my experience is that you do not even need that much to be very comfortable. However, if you set your number too low, then you run the risk of running out of money down the line.

This is where cashflow forecasting and understanding the psychology of money suddenly become very interesting to you. Once again, you can do this on your own, although I would strongly recommend that you consult with someone who is familiar with this type of planning. They should have significant experience in dealing with people at this stage in the business cycle. It is far too easy to get emotionally involved with your own money. This rarely produces the best decisions. You need someone who is not emotionally involved in your financial situation to help you figure out what monetary success means to you.

Using cashflow forecasting, it is possible to come up with a figure – your number – which is the amount of money that you need to achieve financial independence. Financial independence is all about having enough money to not need to go to work. It allows you to make decisions that are best for you rather than having to follow the money. It gives you the financial freedom to be in control of your own destiny.

So just how much is enough?

I had one client, a few years ago, who sat in front of me and said that he never wanted to go into work again. I suggested to him that the only way that he could do this would be to sell his house and to downsize, and he went away with that thought in his mind. A week later he called me to say that he had sold his house, and asked what to do next. At that point I checked my calculations and we agreed that he was now in a position where he no longer needed to go back to work. He moved to his new house, gave up work and loved his retirement.

Other people may have more financially demanding requirements. I usually find the figure for most people is between £5 million and £7 million, which gives a significant income on an ongoing basis and a sizable buffer if things do not go according to plan.

A few years ago, another client came to me saying that he wanted to sell his business, put his children through private education, buy them properties and not work again. When I asked him what he expected to get for his business he said about £2.5 million, which I informed him was not enough to fund the lifestyle that he was describing. So, we simply went back to the drawing board, looked again at what he really wanted out of life and agreed upon the number that he needed to achieve before selling his business.

It is important to speak with someone who deals with the large figures that I hope you are aiming for on a regular basis. You do not want to be your advisor's largest client. You want it to be a matter of course so that they clearly know and understand what needs to be done at the relevant time.

SHOW ME THE MONEY

Now that you have successfully negotiated setting up and running your own business, and have planned for the future, you have reached the final part. The sale.

This is the last stage in monetising your ideas and hard work and finally securing your financial independence. Once again, as soon as you start thinking of selling your business you need to get the right advisors in place. The right advisors will have dealt with these situations many times before, will proactively guide you in the right direction and will hold your hand through the whole process.

In fact, they will make it all look so easy that you will wonder why you paid them so much money for their professional advice. However, if you do not get the best then not only will you end up paying more money, but you will also start to understand how complicated it is to get everything right. Like all the best people in professions, sport or any other discipline, those who are good at their job make it look very easy.

You want to be working with someone who you know well, who you have worked closely with for at least a couple of years, and who understands you and your approach to money. You need a plan in place to make sure that you have all the angles covered, with wiggle room so you can make changes at any point if need be.

Financial independence gives you freedom and brings you opportunities that would not have presented themselves previously.

In fact, we often find that the successful sale of a business is not the end of someone's career, but merely the start of another, where they have the opportunity to make even more money than from their original endeavours.

It is also about getting used to the money. A number of times I have heard people say that their new-found wealth will not change them at all, only to find a couple of years later that they have made that visit to the Aston Martin garage, followed by a visit to the jewellers for some expensive watches and to the estate agent for a new house.

A good financial plan should be able to take these changes into account: the purchases are a sign of the new-found financial flexibility that wealth provides. You deserve your financial success. You had the guts to set up your own business, the determination to make it work and the foresight to maximise the financial benefit from your success.

Your financial planning is part of a complex matrix that will enable you to maximise the benefits from the success of your business. Getting the right advice from a wide range of professionals that you trust is the best way to leverage your time and ability. There is no benefit in being financially well organised without the right legal or accounting advice.

It is also important to understand that getting the right accountancy advice is different to getting the right financial planning advice – both disciplines should dovetail seamlessly to create a forceful synergy that covers all areas of your finances.

TAKEAWAYS

- Having the right kind of financial advice at every stage of your business journey will ensure that you avoid common pitfalls and make the most of what your business has to offer.

- Whatever turnover figure you think you are going to achieve in your first year, halve it. And double the length of time you think it is going to take to set your first business up.

- In the first growth phase, HMRC will go from being a minor to a major cost. Having a proactive accountant who works *with* your business can help with this.

- When you are approaching the sale of your business, get help from an appropriate financial planner to figure out how much money you need in order to achieve financial independence and the lifestyle you want to lead.

- Finally, during the sale process itself, having the appropriate advisors will ensure that everything goes smoothly and you can move on to whatever the next phase of your life brings!

15

LEGAL BUILDING BLOCKS

JONATHAN DAVAGE

INTRODUCTION

'Diligence is the mother of good luck.'
(Benjamin Franklin)

It is 8.30 pm-ish (the vortex of a company sale completion meeting can distort time somewhat) on a clement (for Manchester) evening in early March 2020. My clients, whom I have acted for since the early noughties, are encamped in our office, deliberating the final points to be agreed before they sign on the dotted line and waltz off into the sunset, bank balances bulging with their thirst for wealth duly quenched. This stack of share sale papers, a foot high, is the culmination of 15 years of blood, sweat, tears, break-ups, fights and a whole lot more: but at last we are here!

Wait a minute… there is the small issue of a global pandemic ravaging through Europe, the US and the rest of the world. 'Just get it signed, or god knows what will happen next week', were the cries! 'Stop pissing around and tell 'em to feck off', was the gist of my instructions…! Such colourful use of language is usual when dealing with the sometimes strange, sometimes marvellous and sometimes dangerous beasts labelled as entrepreneurs.

So we proceeded, closed the deal and sped off to the nearest tavern, exhausted, elated and fulfilled.

The above is an example of the endgame for any owner: the sale. The windfall will give you choices in life. This could be to dive into another startup, take some time out, or do something completely different. Financial freedom is not the sole meaning of life, but it does allow you the time to consider your options, and gives you the confidence to go on your next adventure.

Starting your own company involves courage, calm, commitment and much more. Even though I have been in the legal business (my firm being quite entrepreneurial) for 20 years, it never ceases to amaze me how different each entrepreneur's experiences and journey (whatever this means) can be. However, there are some basic pillars from a commercial legal perspective that can make your progression away from the garage, bedroom, coffee shop or even above a chippy much easier and save you a lot of stress and hard-earned cash.

No one can predict the future or anticipate when problems will arise, but you can certainly set down some markers and wayfinders by taking the legal framework of your business seriously from day one.

In this chapter, I will set out some of the most common mistakes I have come across relating to startups and suggest proactive solutions to avoid these, or to at least be ready if issues arise, which they will. All companies have growing pains, some more than others, and it is an owner's ability to weather these storms and ultimately turn a negative into a positive which will set you apart. Having the correct legals is part of the solution (think of it like insurance) and should not be underestimated. Well-drafted legals give you negotiation power and avoid ludicrous legal bills or spending countless hours trying to understand what our learned friends in nice wigs actually mean – in other words, you should avoid court at all costs: there is rarely a winner!

A FEW THINGS TO TAKE NOTE OF IN THE EARLY STAGES OF YOUR BUSINESS

1. **Don't be scared of professional fees**: negotiate, spread the costs over a period, or cap them, but stand behind them. Any smart professional will expect (quite rightly) to be paid for good work, so get decent advisors. As my dear mum says, 'You get what you pay for' or 'If you buy cheap, you buy twice!' Getting bad lawyers/accountants could end up costing you a fortune in the long run, so choose your team wisely.

2. **Assuming trust/competence**: trust needs to be earned, so don't be wooed just by a non-executive director's impressive CV. A lot of CVs are loose with the truth! I have seen equity given away far too easily before the promised goods have been delivered. Work with people for a while before fully committing.

   There is no substitute for working with somebody face to face. CVs, although a good starting point, should always be treated with caution: they do not tell the whole story. This principle also goes for your co-founders. You can have all the legal documents in the world, but trust and integrity outweighs all. You need to be confident with your founders before jumping in.

3. **Google law!**: there may be solutions on the web, but get proper legal advice. Templates and downloaded legal documents can lead to disaster.

4. **Intellectual property (IP)**: get this vested in the company from the start; this and your management team are your main assets. Don't leave any loose ends: make sure founders assign IP, along with consultants and service providers.

SETTING UP THE COMPANY AND SHARE STRUCTURE

INCORPORATING A COMPANY

The first step in any startup is to form the business vehicle. A private company limited by shares is the most common vehicle. Here are some advantages of using this structure:

- Has a distinct legal personality separate from its founders. The company enters into contracts with third parties and employs staff; this is a requirement by finance providers when taking on debt, equity etc.

- Ring-fencing of personal liability, so you can protect your home and other assets.

- IP can be pooled and protected in a non-trading group company. IP property developed with a group of colleagues will be owned by the company and shared by equity to avoid disputes.

Any choice of business structure should be actioned after seeking tax advice from your accountant.

SHARE STRUCTURE

'You can't unscramble eggs.' (JP Morgan)

Having a clean share capital table is the cornerstone of any startup/growing company. This is easy at the start as there may only be one to three founders, but as funding is raised or there is a need for monies, the issue of new shares can get out of control.

Swapping shares for services (known as sweat equity) is a very useful way to obtain services, but always ensure these relationships are documented so the board knows exactly how many shares are in issue or have been promised via an option to acquire shares. This is one of the most common mistakes that early-stage businesses make. Enthusiasm and sometimes misplaced trust leads to undocumented deals or documents not being properly dated/executed. The last thing any founder wants is skeletons in the closet with regards to share capital. So discuss with your lawyer if you are thinking of issuing equity, agree terms in heads or a letter and fully document it, or, if the deal does not proceed, ensure there is no open offer or comeback from the prospective shareholder.

Late-night deals (helped on by bar room board meetings – look at the mess with Sports Direct and the offer of shares after 10 pints!) or errant emails promising x, y and z can become serious issues in the future, so always seek counsel before giving away valuable stakes. Although your business may not be valuable at the start, 5% could be a lot of money at the end, so protect it!

Equity should follow the people who are adding value to the company for a sustained period, not just at the start. Yes, you need to give some away, but do so with caution. People need to earn your trust and respect, which can be rewarded with equity. Cut through the noise and make people back themselves. If services are being offered for shares, work on when the shares are issued, which should be after the delivery of the service, not on day one.

When someone leaves, you need a clear way of getting their shares back via legal documents (see the section 'Shareholder agreement and articles of association' below for more detail).

EXAMPLE

Be cautious of 'share buy-backs' by the company. Simplistically, this means the company purchases shares off a leaving shareholder which are then cancelled and no longer exist; this increases the remaining shareholders' stakes as there are fewer shares. If this is not done correctly, the buy-back can be void, which means the shares are not cancelled and remain in the hands of the leaving shareholder – i.e. a 'phantom shareholder'. This can be catastrophic: as time goes by, the shares increase in value… cue an equity investment/sale and the buyer's lawyer spots this. You are then left in a scenario where you may have to contact the old disgruntled shareholder to sort the mess out. Not a place you want to be! Get advice every time shares change hands.

SECTION SUMMARY

When it comes to funding rounds, if you can't demonstrate who owns shares in your business in whatever guise, you won't get past first base with an investor. Ensure your lawyers/accountants/board always know exactly where the cap table is at.

Common mistakes:

- Equity parted with too easily.

- Disorganised share tracking and documentation.

Solutions:

- Collaborate/work with people for a period before awarding equity, and document any such offers/issue of shares; store this information and have all the dated and fully executed documents.

- Use lawyers when dealing with your share structure, not web-based solutions or accountants. One size definitely does not fit all scenarios, especially as the business grows and becomes more complex.

SHAREHOLDER AGREEMENT AND ARTICLES OF ASSOCIATION

At the core of company law is the Companies Act 2006: this contains thousands of sections, but due to our free market economy, it does not seek either to protect owner managers or to restrict them massively. So comes the need for a 'shareholder agreement' and 'articles of association', but what are they and why are they so important?

A shareholder agreement is a private contract between all shareholders of a company, with the aim of regulating their relationships, rights and obligations, as well as the daily operations of the company. It sets down rules which if breached by a shareholder give recourse against the company or the offending shareholder. It is important to note that shareholder agreements are independent contracts, which means that they are a different type of document that can co-exist with the articles of association of a company.

Articles of association are a contract (in the public domain and filed at Companies House) which regulate the internal management of the company and how power is shared between the shareholders and board. Articles also deal with share ownership, transfer, new issues of shares and exit of individual shareholders and the sale 100% to a third party.

They go hand in hand with the shareholder agreement, and each can contain the relevant protective clauses. For simplicity, the shareholder agreement and articles will be referred to together as the 'equity documents' for the rest of the chapter, as clauses that provide corporate governance, shareholder protection and share ownership regulation can be included in either or both the shareholder agreement and articles of association. The equity documents are bespoke to your situation, so careful thought is required in conjunction with your lawyer.

WHY ARE THEY IMPORTANT?

The startup, seed and growth stages can have many ups and downs, so the equity documents are important because they act as a framework to provide solutions to problems that can negatively affect the progress or growth of the company. The equity documents won't prevent a problem by themselves, but they regulate how this problem can be fixed and what actions can be taken to solve it. *The key here is being proactive and managing your legal framework from day one.*

Think of the equity documents as your charter and legal insurance policy which promote and ensure good corporate governance to potential investors and protect the value of the company should there be a falling-out or if a founder leaves.

Donald Rumsfeld once stated that:

> 'Reports that say that something hasn't happened are always interesting to me, because as we **know**, there are **known knowns**; there are things we **know** we **know**. We also **know** there are **known unknowns**; that is to say we know there are some things we do not **know**.' (Emphasis added.)

At the start of a business, founders will get along and they may not see the need for equity documents as they have not yet experienced any problems. **But you need to be realistic**: problems will arise between you all at some stage which you could not have known about at the start!

The equity documents try to address the '**unknowns**' or '**what-ifs**':

- What if a founder leaves the company?

- What if a founder sets up in competition and takes confidential information or code?

- What if a new shareholder is needed or equity needs to be awarded to your rising stars?

- What if a founder is not dedicating enough time or finds another job?

- What if a founder is not committed/pulling their weight?

- What if there is a falling-out between the shareholders?

- What if there's a deadlock situation?

For all of the above questions and for many others, the equity documents act as a guide and a framework that allow meaningful negotiations and resolution by a pre-agreed legal document. Without them, if a dispute arises, you are at the mercy of the Companies Act (which doesn't give you much help), or worse still the courts, where disputes can drag and become a real thorn in your side. Spending money on the equity documents at the start can save a lot of money down the line.

TYPES OF SHAREHOLDER AGREEMENTS

Equity documents vary significantly depending on what stage of the life cycle the company is at. However, there are three key stages during the cycle where equity documents are essential.

Seed stage

At this stage, only the founders are shareholders, and this could be pre-revenue and before the MVP has been achieved. So essentially the equity documents are in place to regulate the relationships between the founders, as fall-outs are common at this stage. You do not want to be in a position where a founder leaves and you cannot get their shares back for a nominal sum. Equity follows management and the people who are committed and adding value. This needs to be reflected in the equity documents. You can't have one founder sitting on a beach holding a large share of the company whilst the remaining founders are working all hours every day!

Early stage

At this stage the company has achieved the MVP and may have started trading, so the objectives of the company will have changed, along with potentially the relationship between the founders.

The company may have taken on a non-executive director (NED) or require equity, or an investor (usually a High-Net-Worth) may have committed funds.

Therefore:

- As the company already has a shareholder agreement, this will need to be varied to take account of the investor, leaving shareholder or new member of the management team.

- The equity documents may also be amended to provide some protections and economic control to the investor, e.g. they can appoint a person to the board or give access to the accounts.

Growth stage – taking on institutional monies – VC stage

This is post-MVP and during early trading. The business model is settled and proven to an extent. At this stage, professional investors or venture capitalists (VCs) will lead the framework of the equity documents by tabling a 'term sheet'. The old equity documents will most likely be superseded, and the new documents will contain balanced clauses between incentivising the founders and protecting the interests of the investors.

The legal process will be involved, but your experience gained from drafting the equity documents in the seed and early stages will stand you in good stead here.

SECTION SUMMARY

Adopt equity documents from the start and engage lawyers to take specific instructions. Avoid templates and saving fees in the short term as this will come back to bite you. Seek accounts and tax advice.

What do the equity documents cover? A shareholder agreement will usually deal with the following key points:

- **Who** sits on the board of directors?

- **How** are decisions made (do some decisions require unanimous agreement or the agreement of a certain number of shareholders)?

- **What** happens in the event of a dispute?

- **How** can shareholders sell their shares?

- **What** restrictions are founders under if they leave the business?

EMPLOYEES

As the company grows, non-founder employees will be vital to the growth of the business. Human capital is as important (if not more so) than your IP, as the IP needs to be delivered by a well-managed, hungry and incentivised team under the founders.

It is important that the rights of both the company and its employees are properly recorded, and an employment contract should be entered into between the parties in order to best protect everyone involved.

The key terms of a contract of employment include:

- The role.

- Date when the employment began and the nature of its term.

- Salary and other benefits.

- Standard hours of work and job location.

It is also essential that the employment contract includes provisions covering confidentiality and ownership of IP. As standard, all IP created by any employee during his or her employment must be fully vested in the company.

Post-termination restrictive covenants should also be included in order to best protect the company's interests, staff and client base. Invest the upfront costs into proper templates so that a standardised and well-drafted set of documents can be rolled out as the team grows.

INTELLECTUAL PROPERTY

IP is the cornerstone asset of any tech business. IP can be created by the founders writing code, where the copyright (same as writing a book) automatically vests in the individual. Similarly, consultants used (personally or via their company) own the IP unless a formal assignment of IP transferring ownership is signed (IP assignment). So great care is needed or may be key when entering into any agreement that involves sharing or using IP, whether it is the founders, the company or a third party.

Tips on IP assignments:

- Ensure your lawyer clearly defines the IP, such as code, product design etc.

- Ensure the correct parties sign the IP assignment – this is a common problem when dealing with academic institutions, so make sure they go through their lawyers.

- Is there any value to be paid, e.g. for the Design Sprint or development services?

The integrity and ownership of your IP is one of the first things investors look at during due diligence, so this needs to be absolutely bolted down.

NDAS

Confidentiality within tech businesses is key to protecting your idea and IP prior to commercialisation. However, keeping things under wraps needs to be balanced with attracting investors and collaborating with service providers: specific confidential items will need to be shared with both of these groups.

Therefore, where possible, a simple non-disclosure agreement (NDA) is advisable. This may not be possible (a lot of investors refuse, as they have so many pitches to look at and they do not want to be restricted), but the company can seek to protect confidential information by clearly stating that any of the information shared is 'confidential' and should not be disclosed to any person without consent.

TAKEAWAYS

- Building a successful business involves hiring staff and advisors to do the things that you either can't do or shouldn't be doing; this includes a good commercially focused lawyer. Choose wisely and keep them on their toes!

- Correct legal structure and corporate governance is essential to attract investment and to hedge against the 'unknowns' and 'what-ifs' – prioritise and review your legal framework at each stage of your business's life cycle.

- When it comes to funding rounds, if you can't demonstrate who owns shares in whatever guise, you won't get past first base with an investor.

- Adopt equity documents from the start and engage lawyers to take specific instructions.

- Avoid templates and saving fees in the short term; seek accounts and tax advice.

- Spend monies on employee templates from the get-go so that a standardised and well-drafted set of documents can be rolled out as the team grows.

- The integrity and ownership of your IP is one of the first things investors look at during due diligence, so this needs to be nailed down.

- NDAs are advisable, but you can use other methods to protect information if the other party refuses to sign. The NDA is more of a deterrent and quite hard to enforce, so always be careful when sharing data.

16

THE VALUE OF A NON-EXEC DIRECTOR

IAN BROOKES

INTRODUCTION

As founders, you get a lot of advice from a lot of people. Investors, professional advisors, customers, employees, family, friends. Everyone has an opinion. Some of it is valuable, most of it is not, and that's the challenge with founder advice: high volume combined with high variability of value.

There's a lot of sincere, well-meaning advice available to founders. If you're not careful you'll end up drowning in a sea of well-intentioned but overwhelming and often contradictory guidance: 'make drastic cuts' or 'don't cut at all', 'pivot quickly' or 'stay the course and hold your nerve'. Someone might suggest one path and a tweak, someone else may push you for more dramatic shifts.

However, several nuggets of advice I received as a CEO in a former life transformed both my thinking and decision-making style, and as a result, the companies I was leading at the time. They were truly valuable interventions, giving great insights and different perspectives from my own, and I couldn't be more grateful. They came from my non-exec directors.

So, recognising the value of non-execs, I think there are four key questions to consider when navigating towards selecting and working with one:

- What are the qualities of a great non-exec, and how do you leverage these qualities?

- Do you have the right psychology for taking advice from a non-exec?

- What are the sorts of situations you seek input on from your non-exec?

- How do you get good advice from a non-exec?

We'll look at all four of these in this chapter.

WHAT ARE THE QUALITIES OF A GREAT NON-EXEC, AND HOW DO YOU LEVERAGE THESE QUALITIES?

Many founders fail to realise it, but you are only as good as the people you spend time with discussing and reflecting upon your business journey. You want a buddy, a sounding board, an alternative point of view. You want a non-exec who has the experience and has had closer proximity to the outcomes you are chasing – but there has to be a 'personal' fit too.

Non-execs are connectors and catalysts, but not a quick-fix panacea with all the answers. Their main role in the relationship is to listen, replay back, present options, and then get out of the way. It should be a frictionless relationship, built and iterated on through meaningful discussion, providing context to the founder's challenges and needs.

The best advisors share a few key criteria. These include being:

- Successful former CEOs and founders in their own right.

- Recommended by a trusted source.

- Natural teachers with mentoring skills to nurture your learning, not simply givers of 'top down' advice.

- Good listeners and communicators.

- Humble and authentic about their own abilities and success.

- Knowledgeable in the domain related to your business.

You need them to commit to you, so you want them to have skin in the game, being personally (both emotionally and financially) invested in the long-term success of your venture and team. You need them to willingly put substantial time and energy into building connective tissue with you, creating an alignment of shared hearts and minds, but with distinct and independent voices. You want their engagement. It opens you up to hearing something important. And their advice can make your startup.

So how do you leverage the relationship to best effect? Define your relationship this way: tell them what you're thinking of or planning to do, and their role will be to back you into a corner and make you fight your way out. I'd define the role as that of a sparring partner, forcing you as the founder to work hard to defend and explain your position.

Come out fighting: you will often already have the best answer to a problem, but a good non-exec will challenge your thinking, force you to justify it, tease out the details of the solution by making you go through it again. With this sparring dynamic, you're able to practise defending your thinking, unpack it, and hone and strengthen your own reasoning.

A good non-exec will avoid simply projecting their own experiences onto you and avoid saying 'This is how it is' rather than 'This is what happened to me', and put it into a context appropriate for you. They will also avoid projecting their past into the present: what worked when they were operating, or when they made their successful decisions maybe 10 years ago, might not work today.

Equally, you want a non-exec who will avoid being overly protective. You want someone who has high emotional intelligence and empathy, but isn't there to win a popularity contest. You want them to be able to put themselves into your shoes, tell it as it is, whilst having one arm around your shoulder as they help bring clarity to your thinking. They're your 'business dad' or 'business mum'.

Underpinning this, your goal should be to establish a real connection. You need to like and trust each other. You have an inner compass, an instinct that guides you. Use this instinct to evaluate the non-exec you're thinking of bringing into the business, working backwards from the future outcome you want together: a mix of critical friend, mentor and Merlin, in a relationship based on alignment of values, camaraderie, and shared but independent thinking.

DO YOU HAVE THE RIGHT PSYCHOLOGY FOR TAKING ADVICE FROM A NON-EXEC?

Founders always face an expectation to have it all — a clear vision for a new product, the chops to impress potential investors, and the business acumen to navigate a startup through the stages of growth. This burden is made heavier by a founder's natural inclination to take on all the challenges that come their way, and retreat and turn inward in the face of jobs to be done.

The expectation is that the founder will 'figure it out' and formulate a winning game plan. But you shouldn't feel that you have to go it alone. High-quality advice and empathy from an experienced non-exec can make all the difference.

Of course, all the usual disclaimers about experience apply: seasoned non-execs who have a full set of badges and scars having personally passed through the wringer of startup turmoil are quick to point out that we all live in singular circumstances. There's no tried-and-true playbook. A non-exec cannot be a silver bullet.

It's true that no one person has all the answers – let alone all the questions – but an ability to effectively seek and hear out different perspectives can make a meaningful difference as founders try to find their bearings and plot a course. The act of collecting and evaluating advice, even if it's ultimately discarded, can guide founders through their journey.

While the non-exec brings their personal history, perspective and experience to the table in a complementary way, it's up to you to decide what questions are relevant, when to listen and when not to. You want to avoid imposter syndrome and keep your self-respect, but still know how and when to take advice. This can be a tricky balancing act.

Picking through the flow of advice, processing it and then acting upon it is mostly about your psychology of how you take advice. We all have many shades of cognitive bias, and Nobel Prize-winning sociologist Daniel Kahneman's book *Thinking, Fast and Slow*, is a great read on this.

You need to try to stand outside yourself to recognise and balance these biases when listening to and judging advice from your non-exec. For example:

- You will favour advice that confirms or anchors your own thinking, or feeds your ego.

- You won't naturally accept advice that is contrary to your own point of view.

- You perhaps won't appreciate advice that is given in a difficult, maybe critical conversation that sees a loss of faith in your own judgement.

Two other points are important here. First, don't get caught in advice paralysis. As Dennis Hightower said, 'There are 13 ways of doing anything, and 11 of them will work. Just pick one and do it.'[17]

Second, actively seek out negative advice or a contrarian perspective from your non-exec (going back to that 'sparring partner' relationship). This isn't something many of us are naturally wired for and can be emotionally difficult, as criticism is the hardest advice to accept.

Never doubt yourself, however; when a non-exec is willing to shred your thinking and explain why, this shows two things: they want to be truthful and they are not afraid to speak their mind. This shows they are a good non-exec and that there is trust and respect in the relationship.

Finally, this relationship dynamic of giving and receiving advice between you and your non-exec is one with many turns. There are relationship consequences for seeking or not seeking advice, and for following or not following advice. Consistently ignoring advice might strain your relationship; if you dislike the advice offered but it's spot on, acknowledge their contribution and admit that they're right.

WHAT ARE THE SORTS OF SITUATIONS YOU SEEK INPUT ON FROM YOUR NON-EXEC?

When and for what do you need input from your non-exec? It starts with you. Never forget that you, the founder, are the single greatest

17 Daily Press, (2019) 'The core habits of world-class startups' 6 February 2019

point of leverage in a startup, so managing your own mind is a key part of your role. Non-execs should focus on areas where they can nudge, not decide.

Your non-exec will help you to consciously switch decision-making modes to ensure you weigh up all the options, risks and alternatives. The wisdom of the crowd typically beats the views of one person. If you are in agreement on a matter with your non-exec, then there is a high likelihood that the decision is the right one and you should play the odds.

The non-exec should be able to offer you a helicopter perspective – see the big picture looking down – as well as a more granular, detailed perspective on the ground. They can contribute to smaller, tactical decisions as well as the big moments of truth.

It can be remarkably efficient to ask for advice on smaller decisions, simply as a check-in. What CRM is best for startups? How to conduct a team planning day? In these types of situations, listen closely and take their advice to ratify your own thinking, then make these decisions quickly and move on.

As a founder, you may be a quick decision-maker day-to-day, but sometimes the big decisions can lead to paralysis as you replay the possible outcomes and consequences over and over in your head, weighing the pros and cons. You can't wait for perfect information.

Take a leaf from Jeff Bezos and how he works with his non-execs. He says he divides decisions into two types: those with lower stakes that can be reversed and those that are mission-critical, bet-the-bank decisions that cannot easily be reversed. For those irreversible decisions, taking non-exec input and advice is important.

A good rule of thumb is to make the decision when you feel you have 70% of the information you need. This means that even on big decisions you need to be comfortable with some uncertainty, right up until the decision is made, and have confidence in your own judgement.

So how do you identify those impactful areas where you could most use your sparring partner? As a founder, your job day-to-day is leading the business. You're probably making a bunch of decisions fairly quickly or effortlessly, but where are you hesitating? Know where you have a blind spot or when you're less certain or confident because something just feels different. Wherever you find yourself stalling, that's where you should engage your non-exec. Even if you're not aware of it yet, it means you need help.

Startups are hard. There are constant trade-offs, uncertainty on prioritisation, varying degrees of risks and unknowns, long lists of what has and hasn't been tried before to crack a problem. A good non-exec will continuously acknowledge that you are the one in the trenches, working through these problems night and day, but also know when to step in and point out your limitations in under-standing the problem in hand.

HOW DO YOU GET GOOD ADVICE FROM A NON-EXEC?

Powerful, strategy-altering 'good' advice is only as good as the ques-tion that preceded it. When asking for advice, you should be on the verge of acting, but may not know how. At that point, it should be less about your motivations to act, and more about how you go about it.

Good advice isn't necessarily 'the right answer'; it can simply be to help you move forward. For example, when the action you need to take is painful, there's a cognitive bias toward delaying. So if you find yourself hesitating on a decision, recognise your potential bias towards not acting, and remember that this is an area where your sparring partner could help.

To get good advice, don't ask what your non-exec did in the past. This question has limited value, because no two situations are alike. Instead, start by framing your situation. Your non-exec will bring their personal experience into the response, but by framing the question this way you avoid speaking entirely about what has worked for other companies instead of what is best for you.

A good rule of thumb is to come prepared with one topic you definitely want to address and a short list of, say, five key questions, the answers to which will get you the clarity you need. Frame your questions as: 'Here's what I've been wrestling with since we last met, can you please think about how you'd suggest approaching this?' That way, non-execs have time to think back on their experience and pull out the most instructive examples and tactics in the current context.

To get good advice, you need to take the lead in the relationship. Even if your non-exec is more experienced, there shouldn't be a student-teacher dynamic. You're not just showing up and sitting in class; this needs to be self-directed learning. Don't just seek 'good advice' – manage that relationship. Own it. Your non-exec's job is to deliver their best to you, but your job is to direct things so that you get the most out of it.

Non-execs make the best advisors because, like therapists, they've seen almost everything and they're equipped to help you deal with it and learn. They will help you with the blue-sky thinking and washing the pots – seeing the bigger picture and the dirty day-to-day jobs. Their 'good advice' can feel especially pragmatic and useful when you're facing a series of fires to put out.

I've developed a simple formula to check the impact of a non-exec, using four key indicators to evaluate whether the relationship is functioning well and if they're providing good advice:

1. Whether or not the non-exec is responsive to your needs on a regular basis.

2. Whether you feel like you 'leap-frog' your knowledge on a topic whenever you speak to them.

3. Every time you walk away or hang up the phone, you feel like you want and need to spend more time with them.

4. They reframe your thinking in a way you hadn't considered previously

TAKEAWAYS

- Choose a non-exec director like you would a spouse: look for compatibility, connectivity and compassion in the relationship.

- The right state of mind for taking advice from a non-exec is a mixture of humility, knowing when to listen and exercising good judgement.

- There's no hard and fast rule on when you'll need input from your non-exec.

- Don't hold back: you're only hurting yourself if you're not 100% candid, vulnerable and transparent with them.

- To get 'good advice', keep things tied to the decisions that need to be made or the solutions that need to be found; you are in charge of asking the right questions.

- Keep evaluating whether the relationship is working well and you're getting the advice you need.

17

ENTREPRENEURIAL WAR STORIES: BADGES AND SCARS

GUY REMOND

INTRODUCTION

Most of what I write about in books and blogs is about the high-growth period in my company's journey. However, in this chapter, I am going to talk about the early days when I didn't have a clue what I was doing, I had no money and my Plan B was going back to my old career working in food retail.

In this chapter, I am going to describe some real-world trials and tribulations of running a tech startup (the 'scars'), as well as some of the high points (the 'badges'). All of the examples I provide are from the first five years of the company's existence. The company I'm referring to is Cake Solutions Limited (Cake), a software engineering business that was formed in 2001 and sold to a large American organisation in 2017. Cake built complex backend systems for and with their clients. Our ethos was to always be at the forefront of technology and software engineering.

WHAT FUNDING?

My business partner Rob and I set the business up without a long-term plan, with no idea about what we were doing and only having £15k of cash as a startup fund. This included the money to pay ourselves, although while my business partner was young and single,

I had a mortgage to pay and family to support. In fact, my son was born on the second day after we began to work at Cake; I took two days off and then got back to it.

When we set Cake up it was mid-2001; the start of the first Dotcom bust! Not a great time to set up a software services organisation with very little capital to play with. However, that is what we did. Looking back I can see that we were tenacious and adaptable, two key qualities for any entrepreneur. We won our initial business from contacts we had made in our previous roles over the years. I then knocked on the doors of all of the offices in Houldsworth Mill, an old cotton mill converted by the council into offices for art and tech startups, where Cake first opened.

It was incredible how much business we won from building these local relationships, work that kept us going for the first two years of our existence. We began with some basic web design projects and quickly offered more complex database-driven websites and applications. Rob and I had fallen naturally into our respective roles in the organisation: I ran sales and the ops side of the business, neither of which I had any experience in, and Rob, who it turned out was a naturally gifted software engineer, built the websites and the backends. He was actually way better at his role than I was at mine.

We took £86k in our first year and £122k in our second, whilst managing to pay ourselves what we needed to maintain our respective lifestyles and largely remain cashflow positive, which wasn't always the case in the preceding years. We also hired three employees over this period.

For me, this represented success: we started with very little cash, we won business from a standing start, we had no qualifications or experience in running any business and we took on our first employees. Definitely a 'badge' in my book.

CASHFLOW IS KING

In the early days, our cashflow was constantly tight; we often used our overdraft to get by. There were two occasions when we were a week or two away from running out of cash and going bust!

One of these times was in 2003. As I mentioned, neither Rob nor I had any experience in running a business, never mind how to market ourselves effectively. It was my responsibility, but other than knocking on my business neighbours' doors and cold calling, I really had no idea. Cold calling in the software engineering game is not how you generate the kind of business we needed.

We had one lead from an organisation called the National Union of Student Services (NUSSL) that we gained following a technical talk Rob presented. We had to win this significant piece of work. Rob was a confident and talented software engineer; he gave the presentation and knocked it out of the park. We won the business, which became a springboard for even bigger projects, and saved the business.

We only experienced one other close call in 2008 during the height of the recession after we won a tender on a significant government project. Because of the size of the project, most of our team were due to work on it. But to our dismay, the project was delayed by three months, which caused a serious cashflow issue.

We were in the middle of the recession, and despite having an in-writing deal for a significant project from the UK government, our bank was unwilling to help. The old adage that a bank is only happy to give you an umbrella when the sun is shining has some truth: never rely on a bank for personalised support unless it suits them. In the end, I took out a personal loan to fund the shortfall. We moved banks and began to grow off the back of this contract, winning new business.

These experiences were definitely 'scars'. However, as per the popular but very true saying, you learn much more from your failures than your successes. The biggest thing I learnt was that I really had to get to grips with marketing. One of the outcomes of that learning is outlined in the paragraph below, which was the prelude to our incredibly effective marketing strategy based on building personal brands. This is outlined in detail in Chapter 12.

We were also reasonably early adopters of email marketing and used this to good effect. It was so successful for us that we actually built our first product, Easy Emailer – one of the first mass email marketing software products – in order to scratch our own itch!

EXPERT CONTENT GENERATION

Cake's mantra quickly became to stay at the forefront of software engineering. In 2002, Rob became interested in a new framework in the Java world called the Spring Framework. It was an open source piece of software that made developing applications in the Java programming language easier. He began spending time contributing to this project and became one of its core contributors.

This was a significant differentiator for Cake, as the Spring Framework gained in popularity and helped ensure we were keeping to our mantra of staying at the forefront of software engineering. We started to win more of the pitches we were going for because we could show how we would give our clients a technological advantage. As a consequence, most of the projects we were involved with used Java and the Spring Framework as their main technologies. The whole team, at that point seven of us, became experts in these technologies.

Rob and our senior engineer, Jan, decided to write a book on the Spring Framework, and APress agreed to publish it (*Pro Spring*, 2005). This was the third book Rob had been involved with (after *Pro Jakarta Struts*, 2004 and *Pro Visual Studio .NET*, 2004) but *Pro Spring* was the first book that was solely written by the Cake team.

It became a bestseller for APress and put Cake on the map. This generated inbound sales calls from companies wanting systems engineered in these technologies. Even if a potential client hadn't read the book, we took a copy to all sales meetings to give to them. Our expertise was then never in doubt, and we were able to focus on closing the commercials for the deal.

The Cake team writing books that were not only published but actually sold well across the world was most definitely a 'badge'!

PUNCHING ABOVE OUR WEIGHT

We had submitted quite a number of bids for public sector projects and never won any of them, despite being eminently capable of delivering a high-quality service that would fulfil the brief at a reasonable cost. The problem with the tendering process is that you can waste an awful lot of time and therefore money on these bids, and then you get the feeling that you never actually stood a chance of winning it for reasons out of your control.

Although I do think things are improving, there is still an over-reliance on the large well-known companies, as they are seen as less risky. I do think there is something in the old adage that 'you will never be fired for hiring IBM' in relation to the public sector. That kind of thinking and culture prevents the much more agile, innovative and very capable smaller organisations from winning contracts, and wastes hundreds of millions of pounds each year. Because we felt the system makes it uneconomical to bid for these projects, our strategy was to concentrate on the private sector which moved much more quickly and made more commercially sensible decisions.

That all changed when we received a call from a government department who had read the *Pro Spring* book and asked us if we would be interested in submitting a tender to build what we would describe today as a platform for their department. We were up against sizable professional service outfits and we won the contract. It had the potential to be the largest project we had worked on to date. We were incredibly grateful for the opportunity and were completely focused on making it a success.

The project was indeed a success and we went on to win a number of other bids for work with that particular government department. It was a win-win: we won significant business over the years from them, and we ensured every project was a success. We proved that engaging with small specialist companies is very often much more conducive to providing value for money to the taxpayer, and is actually *less* risky!

I am sure we would not have been taken seriously if it wasn't for the book – it demonstrated our expertise. I was speaking to a civil servant who was involved in the project; he had come from a department who only ever used the big names and he admitted he was nervous about working with such a small company. After the project he told me he would never work with one of the big outfits again; we had genuine expertise and really cared about the outcome. This was most definitely a 'badge'!

LOSING A LIMB

Cake was formed in 2001, and in 2006 my business partner left to pursue another opportunity. This was a major change and something of a body blow for the business which could have been catastrophic.

As I mentioned above, Rob had become a core contributor to the open source Spring Framework. The software architect who started the project had been speaking to Rob for 12 months in an effort to get him to join a company he had formed to provide consultancy and engineering services around the Spring Framework. It was a great opportunity for Rob, and I understood his decision in the end to make the move; he is still a friend to this day.

However, up to that point, we had relied heavily on Rob to lead the engineering side of the business. This responsibility to lead the team fell on Jan, our senior engineer at the time, who subsequently became our CTO. We not only managed to carry on; we in fact slowly began to grow the business, ironically off the back of the success of the Spring Framework and the resulting demand for engineering services around this. It forced everyone to up their game, and we all rose to the challenge.

Losing a business partner who is pivotal to the company is a blow to the business but isn't an automatic nail in the coffin. It led to other people in the company stepping up and allowed them to begin to fulfil their potential more quickly than they may have done otherwise. Losing a key business partner was a 'scar'; however, it taught me and other members of the team so much, and gave us the confidence to rise to future challenges.

THE LARGEST CHEQUE

One of the KPIs I used to measure how well we were doing was the size of the 'largest cheque' – in other words, how much a project was worth. Throughout the evolution of Cake, the largest cheques got bigger and bigger. This happened slowly at first, but as our notoriety grew so did the project size. Also, our day rate rose as the demand for our services increased, which meant our project profitability grew.

There were five notable occasions when the size of the largest cheque rose substantially. Every time this happened we used the improved financial position to grow the company. This was deliberate and opportunistic, but not without its risks.

Bringing in such big projects often engaged most of our resources. For a period of time, we became reliant on one client. This is not ideal and carries substantial risk if, for whatever reason, a project ends unexpectedly. However, we used the finance generated throughout the project to hire more great engineers. We also used the time that we were involved in the project to keep increasing our profile and exposure to the market, which created new sales opportunities. How quickly we did this equated to how quickly we minimised the worst of the risk.

Business success is all about making some (not all) great decisions with a healthy slice of luck. By making informed bold decisions and mitigating as much risk as possible, you give yourself the best possible chance of succeeding. Over the years, with this in mind, you will gain your 'scars' and 'badges'.

TAKEAWAYS

- Being tenacious and adaptable are two key qualities for any entrepreneur.

- Cashflow is king: stay on top of your marketing to keep new work and clients coming in, and if possible don't rely on the bank for personalised service, because you may not get it.

- Build up capital in the business that allows you to deal with the ups and downs of business without relying on anyone else.

- Demonstrate your knowledge and skills to potential clients with expert content generation.

- Losing a pivotal business partner can be a blow to the company but isn't an automatic nail in the coffin.

- Use big financial wins to grow your business; make bold choices while mitigating your risks.

18
CLOSING THOUGHTS

Getting a startup off the ground requires a great deal of moving parts. We started by exploring how entrepreneurs need to think in order to create a startup strategy that combines disruptive and disciplined approaches, much like combining the art of playing poker with the art of playing chess.

Startups need to have the ability and discipline to execute strategy well, and entrepreneurs need to understand that every decision is a bet that commits you to a course of action while eliminating the alternatives.

Takeaway: Hope is not a strategy, but a strategy gives you hope when faced with the unknown. Startups need to be comfortable navigating in unknown and uncertain territory, and a strategy is essential for success.

Tech startups are born out of ideas for tech products or services. Whatever your aim, you'll need to start with a minimum viable product (MVP). When done correctly, this becomes the first part of a never-ending roadmap for product development, one you can build and iterate on.

Takeaway: Remember the word 'minimum' in MVP. Prioritising ideas is not the same as devaluing them. Be realistic about your initial user/data volumes and save time by incorporating tactical and interim solutions into your early releases.

In addition to a realistic MVP, you also need a vision for your technology and a product roadmap to guide the iterative process and enable you to innovate in the long term. A product roadmap is an evolving document that sets out what you will do, motivates your team and improves communication between the founder, the team and key stakeholders.

Your technology vision is about how you develop your tech thinking to deliver on what's featured in the roadmap.

Takeaway: Start small but think big. Make sure your product roadmap goes beyond your MVP and that you think about the key technological aspects of your project early, from what programming languages, frameworks and tools you'll use, to your mobile and cloud strategies for product development and scaling the business.

Our Startup Sprint© approach combines various tools to help you ask and answer critical business questions. It's a methodology that puts the Lean Startup ethos at its core with the aim of moving thinking into doing. As a startup, you need to set big, unrealistic goals and then work backwards to achieve them, just as Kennedy did when he announced America's moon landing mission.

Takeaway: A startup is about testing your hunches and taking calculated risks. By breaking down a big goal into smaller steps, each becomes achievable and you have the ability to pivot as circumstances change. Our Startup Sprint© methodology will help you develop a high-level business strategy and plan to take your startup towards its moonshot.

In a tech startup, it can be challenging to find the right software architecture that walks the line between the fast-paced environment you're working in, the need to pivot, and the structure required for scalability in the long term. Even if you're not a techie, it's still important to understand the key architectural characteristics of your tech product.

Takeaway: Think about your software architecture early and consider it a set of clear and simple blueprints that your engineering team can use to build a stable and long-lasting system that has responsiveness, resilience and elasticity built into it.

Cloud technology has changed how we think about computing and opened many doors to startups that were previously closed. Making best use of this technology can only aid your startup. We introduced the main cloud computing options available to help you find the right one (or ones) for your startup.

Takeaway: Cloud offers more than infrastructure and compute-resource on demand. Startups should make full use of managed services within the cloud to advance their tech product development. Remember, there's no need to reinvent the wheel. Use cloud services where you can, rather than unnecessarily building internal capability.

Once you have considered all of this (and plenty more), your tech startup will (hopefully) be off the ground. The next step is therefore delivering with your tech product or service.

Making the right choices about the technology for your startup includes many elements: language selection, libraries and components, and software architecture among them. When choosing technology, consider how easy it will be to find developers with the right knowledge and skills on an equal footing with the technology's capabilities.

Takeaway: Always look to the future when you're making your tech selections, both in terms of your future team and the future of your product. Plan your application with flexibility in mind to enable you to adapt to both business and tech changes.

Just as important as the technology you choose is the process you follow to develop your tech product. Due to the continuously changing nature of the tech landscape and consumer needs, your product will constantly need to evolve to keep up. The key is to design a process that reflects this.

> *Takeaway: Refactoring and maintenance activities offer more benefits than you may initially realise and will save you time in the long run. Invest in automation early to give your developers the confidence and ability to make changes to your product quickly.*

Having a great tech team to support your startup is just as, if not more, important than the technology choices you make. However, the two are closely related. If hiring a world-class team isn't an option, consider the benefits of finding a technology partner instead.

> *Takeaway: Your tech team is the heart of your tech company. Encourage a culture of continuous learning by hiring seasoned engineers alongside less experienced developers and support all the members of your team to learn and improve their skills.*

Once you have your team in place and have chosen your technology, you need to focus on your process. This is challenging to get right, but fundamental for successful and efficient operations, and is where our Startup Sprint© comes in. It's also important to follow the values and principles of an agile process.

> *Takeaway: Choosing your process is just the first step. It's important to iterate on your process as well as your product. Follow the cycle of build, measure, test, learn, repeat.*

Your technology and process feed into the culture of your startup, and a well-structured cultural platform can be the foundation you need to drive growth. There are many other aspects that feed into your culture and that are no less important than tech and process. These range from the people you hire and the environment you create, to the tools and resources you provide, as well as the perks and benefits you offer.

> *Takeaway: Your culture is what will make you stand out from your competitors and what will enable you to hire the best talent. A culture of continuous learning and development should be baked in. Don't only focus on technical skills; soft skills development is just as important.*

Once your startup is up and running, you need to focus on your long game. Many of the recommendations made in the final part of the book can be implemented earlier in your startup journey if that's appropriate. Among those is marketing.

As a startup, you don't need a huge marketing budget if you approach it in the right way. One of the most effective ways of marketing your company is to encourage your team to build their personal brands by sharing expert content about the technologies you use and the projects you're working on.

> *Takeaway: Build the concept of personal brand building into your culture and support all of your team to take part if they want to. Sharing expert content in this way acts as a strong sales tool, pre-qualifies leads and can help you attract some of the top tech talent to your team.*

Finding a good accountant, ideally one who can be a finance partner, with the right ethos to support your startup is essential, and a step you should take as early in your journey as possible. In the early days, working with an accountant who provides advisory services alongside their core financial skills is highly beneficial. Eventually you want to find a finance director for the strategic approach required for long-term growth and success.

Takeaway: Finding the right finance partner will instil a positive financial mindset throughout your business and enable it to perform better in all areas. It will free you up to focus on the business, rather than becoming bogged down in financial matters.

While the finances at your startup are undoubtedly important, so too is your personal financial situation. Make sure you have reserves to support your new business, which you will certainly need, as well as taking the time to thoroughly understand your cashflow.

Takeaway: Having the right kind of financial advice at every stage of your business journey, both personal and professional, will ensure you make the most of what your business has to offer. Good financial advisors with experience of business sales and acquisitions will be more than worth the money you pay them in the end.

Having the correct legal advice to support your startup will pay dividends and should not be underestimated either. Seek professional advice on how best to set up your company and its share structure. Be proactive and manage your legal frameworks from day one, which applies to every area of your business.

Takeaway: A commercially focused lawyer will be invaluable in every area of your startup. Their advice can ensure your company is able to attract the investment it needs, protects its IP and that the rights of both the company and its employees are properly recorded. Cutting corners in legal fees during the early days will almost certainly cost you dearly as your business grows.

Specialist advice for startup founders isn't limited to the financial and legal. There can be a lot to be gained from working with experienced non-executive directors too. However, it's important to understand the nature and dynamic of the relationship you need to form with your non-execs, one where you can both be completely open and talk constructively when you take opposing points of view.

Takeaway: Developing a valuable relationship with a non-exec will take time and effort on your part. You also need to cultivate the right state of mind for taking advice. Remember that your non-execs are there to advise you, not to make decisions for you.

As an entrepreneur you will earn badges and scars from running your own business. Although the badges make you feel great, it is often the scars that you learn the most from. Being adaptable and tenacious are key qualities for any entrepreneur, and you need to focus on your finances as this is where many startups come undone.

Takeaway: Learn from the badges and scars of the entrepreneurs who have gone before you, as well as collecting your own.

This is where thestartupfactory.tech can help. We are experienced entrepreneurs, engineers and developers who have our fair share of badges and scars between us, as well as a passion for helping tech startups turn their vision into a reality.

Through this book, we've shared our knowledge and expertise, as well as that of some of our key strategic partners. What you've read in these pages is an overview of the many business aspects you'll need to consider to become a successful tech entrepreneur. Please use this to support your own startup, and reach out to us if you would like further advice or support. You can contact us at hello@thestartupfactory.tech

ABOUT THE AUTHORS

SIMON BOOTH

Simon has over 30 years of experience in financial planning, both working in the corporate financial world and then running his own business, Foresight Wealth Strategists, where he advises business owners, professionals and high-net-worth individuals.

Having founded his own business in 1998, he knows about the trials and tribulations of entrepreneurship and understands the need to pivot and adapt as economic circumstances change. Simon is a trusted advisor to thestartupfactory.tech, where he shares his years of valuable experience and knowledge with a new generation of entrepreneurs.

IAN BROOKES

The founding father of tsf.tech, Ian has spent the last decade working as a co-founder, investor and board member/advisor with a number of tech businesses and startups, incubators and university spinouts. He has hands-on fundraising experience in excess of £60 million via PLUS, AIM, FTSE, VC/PE and Angel Investors.

Prior to this, after eight years with PW, he was founder CFO at an IT Services business, taking the business to a FTSE listing, and latterly spent five years as CEO. In this time, the company grew from an £18 million private company to a £250 million turnover plc. Ian has a research and teaching interest in entrepreneurship, and delivered entrepreneurial learning programmes as curriculum designer, lecturer and tutor on MBA programmes at Manchester, Lancaster and Sheffield University Business Schools. He currently helps guide the tsf.tech startup portfolio in their growth and scaling phases.

JAMES BROOKES

James is Head of Projects at thestartupfactory.tech. He cut his project management teeth working on tech startups in an open source environment, before working with a leading software development consultancy in the UK, including a period working and living in New York. His role at tsf.tech covers commercial, planning, testing and investor aspects of the startup journey.

James is also the architect and owner of tsf.tech processes, crafting our own version of the agile manifesto, developing a unique user-centric approach based on design sprints and epics to unpack and evolve startups' product thinking.

ERIC CARTER

Eric is Head of Engineering at thestartupfactory.tech and he likes nothing more than rolling up his sleeves and getting stuck into some clean code. He has a strong understanding of the engineering process, helping startups turn their ideas into reality.

Eric studied electronic engineering and then spent a decade developing applications in telecoms, law enforcement and maritime domains. From tiny one-man-army proof-of-concept projects to multi-year international projects delivering enterprise applications, he has seen a lot of variety but also a lot of similarity and boiler-plate code. He is an advocate of agile and iterative development methodologies, as well as dev-ops.

JONATHAN DAVAGE

Jonathan is Head of Corporate at Bermans.. He has spent his legal career advising SMEs and is a specialist in transactional and corporate finance work, as well as providing general strategic board advice.

Jonathan has worked with clients across a range of sectors, but has particular expertise in financial services and technology. Jonathan is a trusted advisor to thestartupfactory.tech, where his knowledge and experience allows him to provide clients with clear direction through what can be quite complex processes.

GUY REMOND

Guy is a founder and Non-Executive Director at thestartupfactory. tech. He was a founding member of Cake Solutions in 2001, following his passion for anything technical. Over 16 years, he directly oversaw the development of the business from a small startup to that of an international, multi-million-pound company respected as being at the cutting edge of engineering and process in the open source software development world.

Cake was acquired by a multinational corporation and the business was subsequently rebranded as Disney Streaming Services, which is a wholly owned subsidiary of a company owned by The Walt Disney Corporation. As a creative and widely experienced individual with a keen focus on personal development, Guy is now able to turn his hand to various non-executive and investor roles both in the commercial and voluntary sector.

ELLIOT SMITH

Elliot is a qualified accountant and experienced finance professional with over 20 years in the industry providing advisory services to startups, entrepreneurs and established businesses. He works with a small portfolio of businesses as an advisor, director and investor.

As Finance Director of thestartupfactory.tech, Elliot provides financial and strategic advice backed up by his many years of commercial and general business experience across a wide range of services and sectors. He brings insight and expertise to the business and its clients, and is a good sounding board offering support far beyond his financial expertise.

ALEKSA VUKOTIC

Aleksa joined thestartupfactory.tech as CTO after a career in the finance industry, where he helped design and build data-driven distributed systems, dev-ops platforms and APIs within the commodity trading and banking sectors.

Prior to that, Aleksa shaped his technology thinking through consulting with organisations (both large corporates and early-stage startups) about how to efficiently use the latest innovations in technology, tools and practices to build quality products and effective technical teams. He now uses his extensive experience to help startups with system design and architecture, technology selection and successful delivery of MVP software products.

THESTARTUPFACTORY.TECH

We're a team of passionate folk who work with tech startups to turn their vision into a reality, enabling tech innovation and customer-centred thinking in everything they do.

We're entrepreneurs, software engineers, designers, analysts, agile practitioners. We're also bloggers, explorers, speakers, swimmers, dog lovers, coffee addicts, campers, walkers, musicians, gamers, footballers, readers, travellers, gardeners, parents and optimists. We bring our true selves to work. Our business is defined by who we are, our values and the culture we create.

You can learn more about who we are and what we do at: https:// thestartupfactory.tech/

APPENDIX

TSF.TECH STARTUP INVESTMENTS

BANKIFI

Sector: Fintech
Co-founders: Mark Hartley & Conny Dorrestijn
Website: https://www.bankifi.com/

Mark's pitch was simple: The bank is the platform; BankiFi is open banking at work.

BankiFi offers 'beyond banking' services, such as invoicing, payments, nudges, cash management and accounting, to businesses. But it doesn't compete with banks, rather it offers the services to banks which can then create bundles to meet the needs of their customers with such features as bank-branded accounting engines at a fraction of the cost a business would pay to buy the software from separate vendors like accounting package providers and niche banking services apps.

BankiFi helps business customers see things through a different lens. BankiFi's approach was to bundle sets of microservices to build the right solution for each business relevant to specific challenges at a specific moment in time. It does this by mining relevant data from multiple sources for actionable insights, giving nudges around liquidity, cash management, invoicing and collections through the 'Request to Pay' service.

BankiFi has become our largest investment. We took the relationship from initial MVP build, through to hiring and building the initial tech team, to CTO-as-a-Service and then helping early customer adoption with technical product support. With two funding rounds secured, BankiFi is well placed to become a high-growth entity in the global fintech marketplace.

NIVO

Sector: Fintech
Co-founders: Michael Commons & Matt Elliot
Website: https://www.nivohub.com/

Mike and Matt engaged with tsf.tech as part of the Barclays Accelerator programme to help build out their business idea, born from their experience of several years in corporate banking.

Nivo is a secure instant-messaging platform for customers to contact institutions and businesses securely and asynchronously, enabling a far wider range of interactions, which previously would have required a customer to go to the business several times with paper-based documents or engage in a lengthy phone call. Nivo removes the need for customers to constantly go through lengthy security questions by saving the customer's profile and identification and verification level (ID&V) across multiple institutions.

The initial engagement began with tsf.tech's CTO providing architecting and design services to outline the solution, before a team of developers, together with the Head of Design and Head of Projects, were onboarded to drive the development forward. The initial development included two third parties – SQR developed the first version of the iOS application (Nivo App), and Callsign who handled the passwords and security aspect of registration and login for customers.

The early web application (Nivo Hub) was built using Scala and the Play framework in a microservices architecture hosted in the Cloud on AWS with Jenkins being used for continuous integration and deployment (CICD). Latterly, under the leadership of Tim Tenant (CTO) and with a successful funding round secured and a strong NED team, the product continues to be developed as a leading-edge solution.

FREEUP WORLD

Sector: IOT
Founder: Dr Tom McNamara
Website: https://freeup.world/

Dr Tom McNamara is a PhD graduate from the Manchester Institute of Biotechnology, having studied biochemistry and materials science. Tom was an enterprising scientist looking to move from academic to entrepreneur, and attended an innovation programme we ran in conjunction with the university. Emerging from this, Tom developed a prototype solution that measured analogue dials remotely. Our first successful test included a tin of beans!

Working alongside tsf.tech from day one, he set up a spin-out company to develop the analogue-to-digital technology which could be used in scientific, medical, industrial and agricultural environments. It was a great collaboration, with Tom's scientific approach supported by our tech skills.

The first product developed was a solution to digitise virtually any analogue dial and so enable workers to remotely monitor equipment that is fixed in their workplace – and be alerted by text if there is an emergency reading. This saved them time and cost – and also picked up measurements not previously tracked.

Current test applications are as diverse as monitoring equipment in a state-of-the-art science institute and a high-tech milking parlour, to manufacturing plants and data collection for water testing in rivers in collaboration with major utility companies. We have supported Tom with additional investment funding and hands-on, hands-in support, including recruitment of his first team.

SOCIAL PLUG

Sector: Influencer Marketing
Founder: Reece Douglas
Twitter: https://twitter.com/reecedouglas1

Social Plug is a social media agency helping businesses generate traffic and sales through influencer-generated content.

Another live project as we launch the book, we were approached by Reece to build an influencer marketing platform to help him grow and scale his existing agency business. With a high profile and track record as an actor, Reece has been involved in campaigns for PlayStation Move and JD Sports, so he is well versed in personal branding and marketing.

The MVP vision is to build an influencer marketing platform that connects and rewards influencers over other offerings, and focuses more on local brands. In delivering this, Social Plug will build a community of influencers supporting user-generated content, agency engagement and become a go-to partner for brands.

Reece has every quality we look for in a tech startup founder: passion, knowledge, self-belief, tenacity and a natural ability to connect with people. The combination of his domain expertise, network and our tech will see us co-create an amazing startup venture.

PLYTIME LEARNING

Sector: EdTech
Co-founders: Ian & Lisa McCartney
Website: https://plytime.com/

Another live project as we finalise the book, Plytime Learning is an EdTech company founded by Ian and Lisa McCartney. We all want to give our children the best opportunities for the future. Their vision is to democratise one-to-one tutoring by providing the most effective tutoring at a more affordable price.

The business provides an online learning platform offering personalised content within a gamified environment, supported by a unique tutoring concept that incorporates video communication.

Having developed their business as an off-line venture and concept tested for a number of years, Ian and Lisa secured Innovate UK funding and approached us to invest in and build an online marketplace for tutors, parents and students to significantly improve the efficiency, effectiveness and impact of personal one-to-one tutoring.

The project offered us the opportunity to develop an EdTech solution and get a footprint in a sector where we had no prior experience. It also enabled us to bring design, frontend, backend and data science skills to the technology solution at the MVP stage. Looking ahead, gamification and AI tools and techniques will be added into the solution.

SPOK'D

Sector: Cycling Coaching App
Founder: Rich Lang
Website: https://www.spokd.com/

Spok'd is an online cycling coach powered by smart algorithms. Founded by ex-professional cyclist Rich Lang and supported by Chris Newton, Olympic medallist and British Cycling coach, Spok'd is the only cycling app that creates a truly personalised training plan. Every week your plan adapts to you based on your training and personal data.

Rich came to us with a working version of his app that he'd launched, but was frustrated with the lack of customer traction and had a desire to reboot the design and features to relaunch the product. We implemented the Design Sprint methodology and, working with current users, tested various redesigns and new features.

Subsequently Spok'd is working with industry-leading tech including Training Peaks, ProBikeKit, Garmin and Strava, and has a strategic partnership with Welsh Cycling. As we publish this book, Spok'd is about to undergo a significant refinancing from an angel investor to enable further product and commercial development.

SPHONIC

Sector: Fintech
Co-founders: Andy Lee & Terry Chow
Website: https://www.sphonic.com/

This was our first startup investment. It all started from a pitch in a meeting room at Manchester Airport. Andy and Terry are highly experienced leaders in regulatory compliance, helping global clients manage fraud and risk. They'd spotted an opportunity for a new tech solution and delivered it over a stream of flipcharts, the coffee flowing. We got their insight, passion and innovation thinking straight away. We still have some of the original flipcharts, several years on.

As with all our startups, we built the MVP of their innovative Workflow Management platform. Developing this further in recent years to a fully-fledged product, based on their years of experience in the RegTech industry, Sphonic's founding team pioneered the approach to augmenting digital insights with traditional KYC checks, providing a sophisticated solution to meet the demands of fast-moving digital commerce.

Today, their Case Management System delivers data visualisation capabilities by enabling real-time assessment of platform and vendor performance, whilst also providing real-time AML and fraud monitoring capabilities via the live Workflow Manager data stream.

All of this has been achieved through astute product development, smart marketing and customer development – and without the usual startup capital funding profile. Sphonic's shareholder base remains predominantly around the founders, friends and family from the early years, showing that growing a startup is all about hard work and customers, not chasing endless rounds of funding,

PAYCASSO

Sector:	Fintech
Founder:	Russell King
Website:	https://paycasso.com/

Paycasso delivers customer verification solutions through electronic verification identification and e-authentication. Paycasso delivers expertise in digital identity and provides a level of trust that is commercially viable.

Paycasso has a unique, patented suite of products (VeriSure™, InstaSure™, DocuSure™ and IdentiSure™) to help customers address these critical challenges whilst managing the corporate and consumer risks associated with impersonation fraud and identity theft.

Working with a commercial but technically astute founder was a first for us, but developed into the perfect collaboration. Prior to founding Paycasso, Russell was Chairman and CEO of US healthcare service provider ZirMed. It was his extensive healthcare experience, coupled with his in-depth knowledge of the issues facing commercial operators and government agencies reliant on remote customer identification, which led to the birth of Paycasso.

Following a series of successful funding rounds, Paycasso has gained a number of high-profile international contracts via its channel partner programme, and secured patents in the US and UK.

FITR

Sector: Health & Wellness Coach Network App
Founder: Rhys Jones
Website: https://www.fitr.app/

FiTR's goal is to encourage people to be active outside of the gym environment. It enables people to develop their own space where they feel comfortable, or that is more convenient, and brings personalised health, fitness and wellness to them.

Whether that is personal training at home, yoga at your workplace or running in your local park, FiTR is about you having on-demand access to the best personal fitness coaches, who are right for you, your personality and your goals. Gyms can be scary places, "Gymtimidation" is very real. Why should you have to go to the gym to meet a personal trainer and why should you be limited to only being able to work with the trainers employed there?

Starting with a Design Sprint, we worked with Rhys on design and testing user journeys across the platform, enabling FiTR users to search, match and connect with the best coach for them based on a host of criteria, including gender, motivational style, personality traits, location, time etc.

In final user acceptance testing as this book goes to press, FiTR is well placed to support the move of many former city workers to home-working in response to Covid-19, no longer requiring the gym as part of their personal exercise environment.

OPENSIDE

Sector: Professional Services Learning & Development
Founder: William Johnson
Website: https://www.openside.group/

Openside designs and delivers advisory, training and executive development for the world's leading professional services firms. Having operated a traditional client engagement model based on face-to-face delivery, working with tsf.tech they identified the need for a digital strategy to scale and grow their business in new directions.

As the professional services market changes, so do Openside's clients' contexts, and the learning and development needs of the individual professionals too – a mobile workforce, focus on personalised solutions, and an 'on-demand' environment.

We have a number of projects in-flight and in-test with Openside, leveraging the Openside brand, relationships, reputation and context into 'high-tech, high-touch' digital and technology strategies which we will unpack over the next 12 months.

We have established a joint-venture organisation to develop the technology and go-to-market strategy, to build upon our initial investment and technology product development.

Printed in Great Britain
by Amazon